D0411286

'Well, it wasn't there when I put the cat out last night'

Published by Oldie Publications Ltd
65 Newman Street, London W1T 3EG

ISBN: 978-1-901170-11-5

Printed and bound in the UK by Butler, Tanner & Dennis Ltd

Acknowledgements
The Oldie would like to thank all the writers, illustrators
and cartoonists whose work is reproduced in these pages.

The Oldie

ANNUAL 2011

'Take a letter, Brother Francis – "Dear Father Sebastian, ..."'

Once again, it's my pleasure to welcome readers to another *Oldie Annual.*

We have done our best to provide a representative cross section of material – regular columnists like Virginia Ironside, Raymond Briggs and James Le Fanu, as well as a number of features, most of which have come to us unsolicited and all the more welcome for that.

I am especially pleased to include the work of some of our best illustrators – the late Paul Hogarth (pages 80–81), the long-serving Robert Geary (pages 38–39) – and a selection of our cover artists (pages 48–49).

To all of them my thanks for their inspiring contributions.

Richard Ingrams

CONTENTS

66

80

72

36

VOTE
I BET I WILLBEAT WILLIAM HILL
38

28

44

16

64
RG

58

11

The Oldie
MAKING A STATE
The Oldie
BOBBING UP AGAIN
48

Modern life

What is... a Digital Denier?

DID YOU PHONE a friend today? Call the theatre to book tickets or nip out to the shops? All seemingly innocent actions, or so you may think. Yet there are some people who never email friends, book tickets online, shop over the internet, or watch YouTube. They don't Tweet or Facebook. Worse, they don't even own a computer. You might even be one of them. If so, you are a Digital Denier and the government would like you to see the error of your ways.

Digital Deniers are the opposite of Silver Surfers. As the internet crashes like a tsunami over their lives, sweeping every daily action in its wake, all they want is to be left alone. They want a life offline, free of hacking, spamming, worms, trojans and cookies, penis enlargement, Viagra and Nigerian fraudsters. It doesn't seem much to ask, and yet it is going to be so much harder than they think.

There are ten million people in Britain who have failed to join the internet revolution. Half of them are over 65. The phrase used for these unfortunates is that they are 'excluded' – a somewhat menacing term which calls to mind New Labour terminology for those irritating schoolchildren formerly known as 'expelled'. But according to a recent report, *Digital Britain,* broadband access should be available to everyone by 2012. As a first step the government has targeted the 'excluded' by appointing Martha Lane Fox, 46, founder of the shopping site LastMinute.com, as 'Digital Inclusion Champion'. Her mission is to get six million people online – half of them in the next two years.

Martha Lane Fox is an inspiring woman, as well as being attractive, clever and modest. After her website was sold for £577 million in 2005 she went on to survive a near-fatal car crash in Africa which led to a long line of bone grafts and a body full of titanium pins. It was this accident, which means she now walks with a stick, that redoubled her enthusiasm for shopping online. She is a persuasive evangelist for the web, pointing out all the benefits that online life can bring. She says the 'web literate' are 25 per cent more confident, and 25 per cent more likely to get jobs. They earn on average ten per cent higher wages and, according to research from PricewaterhouseCoopers, the average family can save £560 a year by using the internet to shop around for deals on energy, insurance and household items.

Yet as well as all these wonders, the otherwise charming Lane Fox uttered a line which, to some, rang warning bells. She said: 'I don't think you can be a proper citizen of our society in the future if you are not engaged online.'

The idea of being disenfranchised by the computer could one day be literal

Her remark went to the heart of the argument from the Digital Deniers. The compulsion to get everyone online goes far beyond ensuring that they can watch the *X Factor* on YouTube or get discounts at Marks & Spencer. Its true motivation lies in the relationship between the government and its citizens. Increasingly, if you don't surf the web you are going to be all washed up.

Put simply, it is cheaper to deal with people online than the old-fashioned way involving paper, people and face-time. You can close Post Offices if everyone gets their pensions and benefits via the web. Banks routinely inform customers that henceforth their statements will be 'paperless' and only appear online. BT refuses to answer *telephone calls* for out-of-service lines, insisting that you report the fault online. Soon online tax returns will be mandatory too. What will be next – no doctors appointments unless you book online? No vote? The idea of being disenfranchised by the computer could one day be literal, as well as metaphorical.

With this in mind, the resistance of the Digital Deniers is hardening. The number of people who say they have no wish to be connected has risen from five years ago. They claim that social interaction, physical activity, even the ability to read, are hampered by increased reliance on the internet. They shudder at the way a computer appears to know everything about you from the moment you type in your postcode. They cite worries about privacy – of having their data accessed by unknown companies and bank statements hacked into. And, in surely the most surreal example, they point to the recent incident when hundreds of people who had bought books for their Kindle electronic readers found that Amazon had wiped them remotely. One day the books they paid for were there on screen – the next they had vanished down the memory hole. And the books in question? It just had to be ... the works of George Orwell.

JANE THYNNE

Olden life

What was... the ITA?

'Who plumbed this in?!'

ROUGHLY FORTY years ago, my two daughters were learning to read at Grace Church School, a small private institution on the eastern edge of Manhattan's Greenwich Village. Grace Church itself was Episcopalian, which may explain the air of anglophilia that hung about the place. In any case, I was startled to discover that the school had adopted a curious new British pedagogical gimmick aimed at teaching them to read quicker and better, called the Initial Teaching Alphabet, or ITA. It involved the use of a special alphabet consisting of 44 characters instead of the conventional 26, and no capitals, just bumped-up small letters.

It was pretty easy to see that the ITA bore some sort of relationship to, if not actual descent from, the spelling reform movement promoted by, among others, George Bernard Shaw, whose wonderful example of idiotic English spelling sticks with me: 'fish' spelled 'ghoti' ('gh' as in 'enouGH'; 'o' as in 'wOmen'; and 'ti' as in 'moTIon'). And in looking into its history my suspicion was soon confirmed. ITA had been invented by Sir James Pitman MP, grandson of the inventor of Pitman shorthand and Shaw's colleague in the movement, as a teaching tool for beginner readers. It offered an unambiguous relationship between symbol and pronunciation. Each symbol had one sound and only one. Of course there had to be a number of somewhat weird new symbols, generally made up of combinations like w and h or i, n and g, which had to be learned along with the remaining conventional letters, but the joy of the system was that once you learned how to say any single phoneme (the technical term for the sound value), it never varied from word to word. No ghoti.

The Ladybird Book of Pets in ITA

Pitman devised his system in 1959. In 1961, twenty selected primary schools in the Midlands began testing to find out whether it worked. It apparently did; children learned to read faster using the oddball alphabet. Where a conventional reading programme introduced a child to only 350 words in his first year, an ITA reader, so it was claimed, could read that many words in a few weeks. Moreover, he or she could with ease read unfamiliar words. Pitman set up foundations to supply information and teaching materials. Soon schools all over Britain, the US and elsewhere were teaching ITA. Even publishers stepped in, hoping to make a shilling. Penguin turned out a whole list in ITA, including a 'lædybird' series entitled *peepl at wurk*. In America the ITA-fluent had their choice of *zip and hiz car* and *the nue hors*, among others. By 1970, beginner readers in 4,000 British primary classrooms were engaged with Sir James's elegantly consistent symbols instead of the frustrating and slippery 'traditional orthography' or TO.

Of course one major catch to ITA was that at some point you had to stop using it and make the leap to TO. ITA advocates vigorously maintained that this was not a problem. American children, it was claimed, moved on painlessly to TO after a year or so of ITA. Moreover, their spelling, which might have been expected to suffer, emerged undamaged. But not everyone was pleased. For some children, the transition to TO was disastrous, and they never learned (or thereafter wanted) to read; for others bad spelling remained a lifelong burden. Inadequately trained teachers compounded the problem. Accents varied. In some places a backlash set in. Doubts cropped up about the long-term advantages of an early burst of reading skill. Sir James's foundations gradually foundered, perhaps through an overdose of enthusiasm. While in America an organisation promoting ITA (mainly for dyslexics) survives to this day, the original passion for ITA now seems to be virtually dead everywhere.

My own daughters, I'm pleased to say, thrived under the regimen. Both became skilled readers and wrote voluminously using ITA symbols. Today neither can remember a thing about it and they can both spell 'fish', so I suppose it did them no damage.

CHARLES ELLIOTT

★★★★★★★★★★★★★★★

ILLUSTRATION BY HEATH

★ Great Bores of Today ★

'... Oh my God oh my God I really can't believe that this is... It can't be happening... I'm so... God... I mean... WOW!... Ever since I was three I dreamed of this moment and now WOW! I really can't... There's so many people to thank beginning with my Mum my Dad who believed in me even from when I was a little girl of three and then everyone who worked on the film who made it all possible every one of them should be standing here with me and a big big big thank you to my wonderful agent Trish Menendez thank you thank you... Oh dear I think I'm going to cry...'

© Fant and Dick

The Queen Mother

The Queen Mum wrapped royal artists around her little finger – including sculptor **MARTIN JENNINGS**

The Queen Mother and Martin Jennings at the unveiling of the bust at St Paul's Cathedral

PHOTOGRAPH COURTESY OF TIM GRAHAM/GETTY IMAGES

Ten years ago I was commissioned by the Friends of St Paul's Cathedral to make a bronze bust of the Queen Mum to celebrate her hundredth birthday. Once every three months I drove down to Clarence House with the working model bouncing about in the back of my pickup truck. She could only sit for an hour at a stretch and it was always something of a business settling her into the revolving chair I'd brought along. I was surprised by how small she was. In order to work at eye level, both with the sculpture and with her, I'd have to spend the whole session on my knees. She didn't seem surprised – perhaps a lot of kneeling is par for the course with royalty.

'Queen Elizabeth has sent you this,' he murmured, 'from her own tea table.' He removed the cover. It contained half a buttered crumpet

Her smallness has stayed in my mind, and as the years recede she gets tinier and tinier in my imagination. She seemed to be dwarfed by her cavernous lodgings. Her entire household staff seemed to drain away as soon as she was occupied with a sitting, and as the house went quiet so her bodily littleness and frailty were somehow accentuated.

I'd been instructed not to speak to her, an injunction I ignored, not least because she herself started chatting straight away. You could never quite tell to what extent her conversation was a form of ironic self-parody, one of the last weapons the old have against the young. She asked me to lunch once and when the first course came in, lent towards me conspiratorially, declaring in a low voice 'It's macaroni cheese. Do you know it? It's an Italian dish.' Which of course led one to imagine that she was some kind of daft old stick lost in the 1930s. It took me a while to realise that at least in part this was a role she amused herself with to counter people's boring and patronising deference. In reality she was sharp as a tailor's needle.

Her conversation was peppered with questions begging required responses. 'Do you like the Germans?' 'Well,' I'd say, hesitating, 'I do have one or two German friends.' Which was plainly the wrong answer as I'd immediately receive a certain look. I'd clearly forgotten they'd dropped a bomb on her house once and had generally proved very tiresome for a considerable while.

At 99 she was as coquettish as you please. You swum in her kind regard as in a warm bath, imagining yourself specially noticed and specially blessed. After one afternoon session 'Backstairs' Billy, her favourite page, brought down a small covered silver dish, bearing it with the reverence a priest would accord the sacrament. 'Queen Elizabeth has sent you this,' he murmured, 'from her own tea table.' Deluded fool that I was, I imagined I was being given a rather expensive present. He removed the cover. It contained half a buttered crumpet.

But I wondered whether she hadn't always made a bit of a thing of getting artists to fall for her. If nothing else, it's a crafty way of achieving the portrait you want. In the dining room were a couple of drawings by Sargent displaying her homely form in flatteringly swan-like guise. Where I was working there hung a painting Augustus John had made of her during the war. He had presented her as a slip of a figure clutching a bunch of camellias. It was very soppy and she loved it. She had clearly delighted in having the flamboyant John come along and paint her. His dangerous sexual reputation had preceded him. But it was he who had ended up overwhelmed by her. She was cheerfully self-mocking in her description of flustered attempts to put him at his ease. John was a bundle of nerves, so much so that she'd ordered a calming bottle of scotch always to be at hand in his painting locker. When that didn't work she had a string quartet play in the next room. He'd finally gathered his courage and told her he'd be able to get on if only it wasn't for that damn racket next door.

Sixty years on and similarly tasked, I was freed from such elaborate treatment. After each sitting she would say goodbye with a smile and move slowly from the room on her sticks. I would sink into a chair. Moments later Billy would sweep in, settle the gramophone needle into an old LP of Noël Coward songs and leave me clutching in my hand a glass of gin the size of a bucket. It was all rather great really.

Plucky Jim

The release of Abdelbaset al-Megrahi in 2009 caused a huge row, but for many the important question has been sidelined: who was responsible for the Lockerbie bombing? **JIM SWIRE**, *who lost his daughter in the tragedy, has spent the last twenty years in pursuit of the truth. Interview by* **MELANIE McFADYEAN**

Jim Swire, a handsome, wiry, slightly gaunt former GP in his early seventies, has become an unlikely hero, battling against powerful players in the dirty business of global *Realpolitik*. Since the December night in 1988 when Pan Am 103 was blown up over Lockerbie, killing his daughter Flora and 269 others, he has dedicated himself to discovering the truth. Nobody but the real bombers, politicians, corporate power brokers and intelligence agents guarding the secrets that protect their interests knows more than he does.

As we sit in the sunny conservatory of the Cotswold village house where he lives with his wife Jane, the carnage and dark intrigue of that horrific bombing seem incongruous. So does the thought that spooks have been hacking into his emails and tapping his phone. The pursuit of the truth has cost him his job and led him to places he'd never have gone to, meeting people he'd never have met, changing the course of what would otherwise have been the peaceful life of a country GP with a wife and three children.

When the blame was switched to Libya, Swire went along with it and went three times to try to persuade Gaddafi to send the suspects to be tried under Scottish law

What drives him on? 'My beloved Flora, whom I absolutely adored,' he says, controlling a catch in his voice as he mentions Flora's name. 'My dear wife Jane realised before I did that campaigning was my way of coping. I couldn't have done nothing, I would have exploded. It was probing all this that saved my bacon. It's a huge advantage, having a wife like Jane and being part of Pan Am 103, a group which has never been at each other's throats.'

Jane wears her understanding well, but says that with the release of the so-called 'Lockerbie bomber', Abdelbaset al-Megrahi, it's time to let it go. One can't imagine Swire letting go.

'I don't welcome the public profile that I've had to assume,' he says. 'I just want to get to the truth about who murdered my daughter. The only weapon I've found against people who are concealing the truth is the media.'

After the bombing, government and intelligence agencies blamed the Iranian-backed Syrian group, the PFLP-GC (it was believed to have been a revenge attack for the Iranian passenger plane shot down by a US warship in July 1988). But when Saddam Hussein invaded Kuwait in 1990, the US and UK governments' Middle East foreign policy changed: they now needed Iran's neutrality and Syria's support, and the blame for Lockerbie was switched to Libya.

Swire and the other relatives went along with it. Swire went to Libya three times to persuade Gaddafi to send two suspects, Abdelbaset Ali Mohmed al-Megrahi and Al Amin Khalifa Fhimah, to be tried under Scottish law. The first time he went was two weeks after indictments were issued against the Libyans at the end of 1991. Only Jane and an Egyptian journalist who fixed up the trip knew he was going. 'In those days of course I was totally credulous about the propaganda about Gaddafi and for all I knew I might be put up against the wall and shot or taken hostage. I was scared shitless.'

He was driven out of Tripoli with Libya's Justice Minister in a Mercedes with blacked-out windows. The car zigzagged between concrete blocks and there were armed guards behind every palm tree. Somewhere in the desert they came to a blank wall which opened, Bond-like, to reveal steel prongs eighteen inches long and a Russian tank. He waited several hours in a room full of Louis XVI furniture before being taken to Gaddafi's tent, under which was a concrete bunker.

He looked, says Swire, like Mick Jagger. He wore flowing robes and was surrounded by female guards with machine guns. They shook hands and Swire said, 'Thank you for seeing me, Colonel.' After exchanging pleasantries about their families, Gaddafi said he knew nothing about the bomb. Swire gave him a little album of photos of Flora including one when she was eighteen months old, about the age of Gaddafi's daughter when she was killed during a US bombing raid in 1986. 'It became a person-to-person interview. At the end of the hour I thanked him and gave him a badge saying "Pan-Am 103: the truth must be known". As I approached him to pin it on his robes, I heard the safety catches of the guns being released, and Gaddafi smiled.' There were two more trips to Libya. The third time, the Colonel was in a bad mood.

Flora's death, though never far from his thoughts or conversation, hasn't extinguished Swire's sense of humour. 'All Gaddafi would do was grunt. So I thought of a schoolboy trick. I kept looking under the table. He couldn't resist but ask

PORTRAIT BY GRAHAM JEPSON

Right: Jim Swire at home with the portrait of his late daughter Flora in the background

me why. I said, "I was just checking that you hadn't got Monica Lewinsky under there." He guffawed.'

In 1992 Gaddafi's continued refusal to hand the men over led to UN sanctions on Libya. After international intervention, including pressure from Nelson Mandela (whom Swire has met), Gaddafi finally agreed to the two men being tried under Scots law in a neutral country. Megrahi and Fhimah were handed over in 1999 and flown to the Hague to await trial at Camp Zeist in Holland. Trade deals were brokered, diplomatic changes agreed and, later, financial compensation paid to the families of the Lockerbie dead.

Swire's influence will have played its part in bringing the men to trial. His efforts to persuade were based on his belief in the Scottish legal system as the world's fairest.

He and Jane rented a fiat in Zeist and Swire attended the trial, hearing all the evidence. But far from underlining their guilt, the evidence convinced him that the two were not guilty. For Swire, the trial was a travesty of justice. It was to be a major turning point.

A man from what he calls the cap-doffing generation, he is not a natural rebel. But he has been disabused of his trust in authority – governments, judiciaries, intelligence agencies, airport security. Seeing their corruption and carelessness has forced this mild-mannered, gregarious man to become a thorn in the side of the authorities.

A man from the 'cap-doffing generation', Swire is not a natural rebel – but he has been disabused of his trust in authority

It is a testament to Swire's integrity that after the trial he publicly changed tack. He now knew Megrahi was wrongly convicted. 'I am after the truth. It may not emerge in my lifetime. But we've done enough – eventually it will come out. It's terribly important that the efforts that we made to get to the truth were done with integrity in the name of justice for the memory of our family members.'

Since the 2001 verdict Swire has pieced together an analysis of what really happened which places responsibility on the initial suspects, the PFLP-GC. He demonstrates how the prosecution case depended on obfuscation and lies. He dwells on the possible significance of a break-in at Terminal 3 early in the morning on the day of the bombing close to an Iran Air office and the shed where baggage for the flight was assembled that night. Withheld from the defence, this information only emerged at Megrahi's first appeal in 2002. Swire explains that the bomb used was designed to detonate by pressure change when the aircraft reached a certain height and that such a bomb must have been put on the plane at Heathrow, and not, as the prosecution had it, in Malta. Other crucial prosecution evidence appears to have been fabricated.

Swire's suspicions were vindicated when the Scottish Criminal Cases Review Commission found evidence of a potential miscarriage of justice and granted Megrahi a second appeal. This appeal, which was due to be heard in 2009, was abandoned by Megrahi shortly before his release.

Swire fetches an envelope. In it is a Christmas card from Megrahi sent in 2008. 'To Jim Swire and family, please pray for me and my family.' In November 2005 he visited Megrahi in prison. Swire feels guilty for his part in what he now says was a miscarriage of justice. It all comes back to his love for his daughter. 'I don't want my daughter's memory associated with an innocent man very nearly dying in prison for something he did not do. Flora would not have wanted her name associated with a horror like that.'

He visited Megrahi in prison again in November 2008. 'We understood each other. He knew that I knew that he wasn't guilty. We had an emotional discussion about how he had come to be in this pickle. We talked about our families. I expressed the hope that he got home to his before too long. I said I had a sense of guilt because I went to see Gaddafi to ask him to allow his citizen to appear in the Scottish criminal justice system. I can't be so grandiose as to suppose it was my intervention that led to him being handed over, but it was all part of it. When Megrahi was visited by a member of the Scottish Parliament in prison he said, "When I go home I want to leave material my solicitors have to Jim Swire."'

This material could be vital to the public enquiry Swire is lobbying for now that the appeal will not happen. Swire quotes the UN international observer at Zeist who said the only way this incomprehensible verdict could have been reached was through 'deliberate malpractice by [Scotland's] Crown Office'. Swire has lost faith in Scottish justice and now talks of pursuing the truth by legal challenge, referral to the European courts, to the Security Council of the UN or to the General Assembly.

Swire's determination is impressive and along the way he's made many friends. But he's no stranger to criticism. The media call Megrahi 'the Lockerbie bomber': a few hours with Swire convince you he is not. And Swire is not alone in his analysis. In his brilliant 2001 investigation *Lockerbie: The Flight from Justice* (available on the *Private Eye* website) the late Paul Foot reaches the same conclusions. One might expect a broadsheet columnist to have taken this well-researched document into account. It seems the *Observer*'s Nick Cohen hasn't, writing in August 2009: '[Swire] lost his daughter and the lack of solid information over the years must have fed the wildest suspicions.' A conversation with Swire and perusal of Foot's investigation would have made it impossible for Cohen to patronise and insult Swire in this way.

Most of the hate-mail Swire has had comes from the US relatives of the Lockerbie dead who accept the verdict. '"How could you go and see that devil incarnate, Gaddafi? Why do you do it? You're a traitor." I write back reasoned emails saying look at the facts. I've never had an answer to a reply to a hate-mail letter. When I visited Megrahi there was antagonism – what's that old geezer doing going to see his daughter's murderer? But since Megrahi's release we've had more positive emails and letters than ever.'

Swire showed me a painting of Flora by the father of her boyfriend with whom she was going to spend that Christmas. Flora wears a white dress and carries wild flowers. 'It captures her vivacity, beauty and intelligence brilliantly,' he says. 'She was studying neurology. She had done her undergraduate degree and after her death we found a letter from Cambridge accepting her on a postgraduate degree. She knew I'd be thrilled as it was my university. I think she'd have told me on Christmas day over the phone.'

You wish for Swire, one of the best, that he would give himself a break. He probably won't. He quotes from John Donne: 'On a huge hill, / Cragged, and steep, Truth stands, and he that will / Reach her, about must, and about must go...'

Tips for Meanies

Every month **JANE THYNNE**, *our resident Mrs Thrifty, imparts some handy advice on how to save money around the home.* *Illustrated by* **MARTIN HONEYSETT**

ZAPPING a lemon briefly in the microwave produces far more juice when it's squeezed. When you've had the juice, use the peel to clean tea and coffee marks from cups. Then run the rind (or chunks of orange or grapefruit) through the waste disposal to keep the blades clean and make it smell good.

GARDEN SNOBS may recoil, but Meanies should embrace the pot marigold, *Calendula officinalis*. A dead-cheap substitute for expensive saffron in paella and risottos, it provides a similar flavour and colour. Just dry the petals in the microwave and grind up. The flowers can also be rubbed on bee stings and insect bites, having antibiotic properties, and if you grow them next to your tomatoes they deter pests.

IN SOME HOMES a sofa covered in cat hair is *de rigueur*, but many Meanies like a more pristine environment. Those who cannot bring themselves to buy hair-removal gadgets should rub surfaces with a damp rubber glove or a sheet of fabric softener, which breaks the static bond that makes cat or dog hair cling.

A SOLUBLE ASPIRIN is one of the most versatile weapons in a Meanie's armoury. Not just for headaches but for your skin. Rub it on a mosquito bite and it will soothe the itch because of its anti-inflammatory properties. Its basic ingredient, salicylic acid, appears in most athletes' foot medication as an anti-fungal. It is also the active ingredient in most anti-dandruff shampoos, so adding an aspirin to your shampoo will control scalp problems. A couple of crushed aspirins mixed with water make an effective facial mask – many skin creams contain exactly the same chemical.

WHEN LASZLO BIRO invented the first ballpoint in 1938, he used a thicker kind of ink that dried quickly. Unfortunately, sometimes the ink gets stuck before the cartridge is finished. When your ballpoint clogs up but you can still see ink, don't throw it out. Running the tip lightly down the rubber sole of a shoe will make the ink run again like magic.

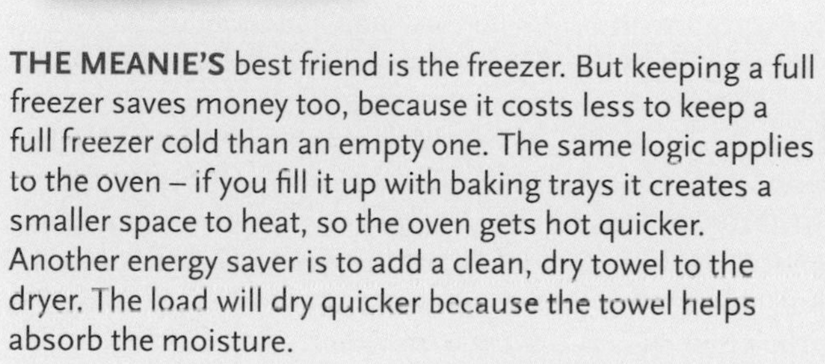

THE MEANIE'S best friend is the freezer. But keeping a full freezer saves money too, because it costs less to keep a full freezer cold than an empty one. The same logic applies to the oven – if you fill it up with baking trays it creates a smaller space to heat, so the oven gets hot quicker. Another energy saver is to add a clean, dry towel to the dryer. The load will dry quicker because the towel helps absorb the moisture.

The Pricke *of* Conscience

Worried about recession, global warming, general doom and gloom? You're not the first by a long way, says **KEN COOPER**

Across the river from York's busy tourist trails, half-hidden between an ugly brick 1960s hotel tower and a vast office block, is a little treasure-house of glowing ancient glass. The windows of All Saints' Church in North Street are among the finest in the world. And one of them has eerie parallels with the troubles of the 21st century – climate change, economic collapse, and the threat of nuclear extinction.

'This is a medieval horror film in stained glass,' Robert Richards, churchwarden and tour guide, tells a party of visitors. 'And be warned – some of this may sound very familiar.'

The 'Pricke of Conscience' window is 600 years old, and forecasts the end of the world in comic-book style: fifteen graphic frames of disaster and death, with captions in Middle English. The storyline is from a bestseller of the times, an anonymous 10,000-line poem of the same name. It must have struck a chord in the medieval mind, for it outsold even Chaucer's *Canterbury Tales*. The story in the windows begins with global warming and rising sea levels. A passage from the poem reads:

The sea shall ryse, as the bukes says
Abouten the height of ilka mountayne
Full forty cubits certayne.

That's around sixty feet, more than enough to change the map of the world. The sea catches fire, then the land, the stars fall from the sky and the fruit drops from the trees. Great buildings collapse, graves open, death gathers everyone, and on the fifteenth day the world goes up in flames – ending not with a whimper but a Big Bang of total conflagration.

All the world shall bryn on ilka side
And the erthe where we now dwell
Until the utter end of all helle.

Robert Richards points out the relevance to current affairs: 'That sounds to me like a nuclear holocaust. As to collapsing buildings, it's not so long since we had an earthquake in Britain. And you can imagine the City tower blocks being shaken to their foundations by the financial crisis.'

Ye seventh daye howses mon fall,
Castles and towres and ilka wall.

PHOTOGRAPHY BY ROGER KEECH COURTESY OF ALL SAINTS' NORTH STREET

DETAILS FROM THE WINDOWS

TOP ROW, FROM LEFT TO RIGHT: on the fourth day, fish rise from the sea; on the fifth day, the sea catches fire; on the sixth day, bloody dew falls from the trees; the seventh day brings earthquakes: 'howses mon fall'; and on the twelfth day, dead men's bones arise
BOTTOM ROW, FROM LEFT TO RIGHT: Donors to the Pricke window look on in horror; the next two frames show the death of everyone on the fourteenth day; the final two frames are from the Corporal Acts of Mercy window, and show a man visiting prisoners and clothing the naked

The window dates from 1410, when wars and plagues were common and life could be nasty, brutish, and often short. Henry IV was king, and the Battle of Agincourt was yet to be fought. People had a real interest in things apocalyptic. From the craftsmen building York Minster to the nobles at the King's court, everyone was concerned where their souls would go on Judgement Day. 'All Saints was a tiny inner-city parish in the 15th century, down near the riverside wharves,' says the parish priest, Father Anthony Horsman. 'The congregation were merchants rich enough to hire the best stained-glass painters around, but also working people, craftsmen and artisans, and most of them could read.'

'They were more in touch with the cycle of the seasons, and death was ever-present,' says Dr Tim Ayers of York University's Centre for Medieval Studies. 'Infant mortality was high, and disease and famine were constant worries. The church offered them a chance of escape to salvation when the world ended. And both the poem and window are written not in Latin, but in the English of the common man for maximum impact. The window has parallels with modern life – you could take that as a sign of the fragility of human aspirations and vanities. It's a horror story, certainly, but it's a positive one – a lesson in what to expect at the end of the world, and how to prepare for it.'

At least it shows we're not the first to reckon the world's going to hell in a handcart

The window seems to bear out the old saying 'What goes around, comes around.' At least it shows we're not the first to reckon the world's going to hell in a handcart. Fr Horsman says: 'People's reaction is usually a muted "wow" – the catastrophes are just the sort of things we see on the news today.'

The window beside it – the 'Corporal Acts of Mercy' – is a contrast in peace and calm. It's a sort of good deeds handbook, showing the corporeal (or bodily) ways to help others. We see a kindly, bearded man feeding the hungry, visiting the sick and welcoming strangers. He's probably a merchant called Nicholas Blackburn, Mayor of York, presumably an all-round good chap, and just the sort to earn salvation at the world's end. Was this also a prick to the medieval conscience – a way of preparing for the future when the whole fabric of society could collapse around you? Dr Ayers seems to think so: 'There was no National Health Service in 15th-century England, and the poor and the sick depended on charity. The message encourages people to help and support others, and earn themselves a place in Heaven. So the two windows can be read together – one's about the impermanence of life; the other about what you can do while you're still here.'

There's one reflection of modern life that the window doesn't show. It comes in the 14th-century poem on which it's based. 'The author ends by saying he's written it in English, because the English are so useless and lazy about learning other languages,' says Robert Richards. 'That was written 600 years ago, and it's something a government minister might have said yesterday.'

Jeremiah McCarthy, shown here in the *Irish Post* on his 105th birthday
© British Library

How I *killed* Ireland's *oldest man*

A life of 'good living, sleep and whiskey' sustained the Irishman Jeremiah McCarthy – until, that is, the dread day in 1974 when he got out of bed to meet **JOHN McENTEE**

Jeremiah McCarthy was Ireland's oldest man. He was aged 108 and lived with his widowed daughter in a thatched cottage in the picture-postcard village of Freshford, in County Kilkenny. In the winter of 1974 I was dispatched with a photographer from Dublin by the *Sunday Press* to interview Jeremiah. We'd been told that he had agreed to be the official starter of a charity walk in aid of the local Mentally Handicapped Society.

At that time it would never cross the mind of a *Sunday Press* team to get in touch in advance. So, fuelled by a few lunchtime jars in Kilkenny, Ray, the snapper, and I arrived at the McCarthy residence on a biting cold afternoon. We tapped on the half-door. It was opened by an elderly lady. 'Are you Mrs Jeremiah McCarthy?' I asked, tentatively. She replied: 'No, I'm his daughter.' Ray indiscreetly gave me the thumbs-up sign. Blimey, we thought, if this old dear is the daughter, then Jeremiah must be as old as Methuselah.

We were invited into the kitchen for a cup of tea. Jeremiah's daughter explained that he had been confined to bed for the previous two years. He wasn't suffering from any particular ailment, but age had slowed him down. Shamelessly, we pleaded with her to get Jeremiah up and out of bed to be interviewed. At the time, the *Sunday Press* was the largest-selling newspaper in Ireland, and the poor dear seemed to feel some obligation to comply with our wishes.

> ***"Jeremiah retrieved his sticks and started the long shuffle back to the kitchen table. 'I'd be a long time walking to Dublin,' he said."***

She agreed and disappeared up a wooden ramp on the kitchen floor into a corridor concealed behind a door. She was gone for about half an hour. When she returned she was accompanied by a small, slight figure wearing a starched grey woollen suit, with creases on the trousers sharp enough to shave by. He clutched a sturdy wooden walking stick in each hand and was wearing a felt trilby, from which strands of white hair peeped out around the ears. His face was adorned with a snow-white, drooping moustache. His eyes were bright and alert. He shuffled down the ramp, relying on his sticks, and slowly made his way to a chair beside the kitchen table.

As I greeted him, his daughter explained that he was quite deaf. 'HOW ARE YOU, MR McCARTHY?' I bellowed. He replied, quietly: 'I'm fine, thanks be to God.' What followed was a conversation peppered with my SHOUTED questions and his mouse-like, mono-syllabic answers. 'TO WHAT DO YOU ATTRIBUTE YOUR GREAT AGE?' I asked. 'Good livin', sleep and whiskey.' At that stage whiskey was produced and his daughter explained that he was a Peace Commissioner – appointed by the Justice Ministry as a person of good character, trusted to witness documents and take statutory declarations – and could still sign his name. A pen and paper were produced.

Jeremiah clutched the pen and tried to make contact with the paper. He missed. His shaking hand hovered here, there and everywhere. Eventually his daughter grabbed his wrist and directed him towards the paper. He wrote in a huge meandering scrawl, 'Jeremiah McCarthy PC'. We congratulated him like a toddler who has just mastered the art of the chamber pot. More questions followed, but he seemed tired.

My photographer started making frantic gestures and brandishing his cameras. 'Would it be possible,' Ray asked, 'to get Jeremiah over to the door so we could get nice shots of him leaning out of the half-door?'

Jeremiah's daughter helped him to his feet and he set out on the long, slow, distant journey to the door. When he anchored himself to the bottom half of the door, Ray was already in place outside on the roadway in the sub-zero temperatures. Jeremiah, sport that he was, smiled and waved, and leaned this way and that. Photographers always require one more. Ireland's oldest man was turning blue by the time Ray decided he'd snapped enough frames. Jeremiah retrieved his sticks and started the interminable shuffle back to his seat at the kitchen table. Halfway there he mumbled something. It was incoherent. 'WHAT WAS THAT, JEREMIAH?' I asked. He repeated it: 'I'd be a long time walking to Dublin.'

When Jeremiah was safely berthed, Ray and I thanked father and daughter and made our exit. The following weekend, the *Sunday Press* carried a sweet picture of a beaming Jeremiah peering out of his front door. The accompanying story outlined his plans for the charity walk. All fine and dandy.

The following day I was walking along O'Connell Street in Dublin, en route to a late shift at work, when I spotted an even larger picture of Jeremiah on the front page of the *Evening Press*. 'What's he up to now?' I wondered as I bought a newspaper. The headline said it all: 'Ireland's Oldest Man Dies.'

It transpired that Jeremiah, safely tucked up in bed for two years, had caught a chill when he was obliged to get up and dress, to pose in near arctic conditions for the *Sunday Press*. To this day I am pointed out by former colleagues as The Man Who Killed the Oldest Man in Ireland. I blame the photographer.

MIND THE AGE GAP

Lizzie Enfield

MY PARENTS were concerned about food miles long before it became fashionable to tell the world you were spending the month eating only things that had been grown within a five-mile radius.

They never refer to food miles as such – they simply have an innate sense of wrong-doing if they eat anything out of season. Were I to invite them for a meal at the end of April, for example, and dish up strawberries for pudding, they would raise their eyebrows and say 'Strawberries!' in a tone suffused with all the moral authority of an Ayatollah.

The implication would be clear: that I lacked the strength of character to wait until strawberries came into season. The fact that the strawberries might have been flown from Kenya in a plane churning out huge amounts of gunk into the atmosphere would be secondary to their concern that I would be eating strawberries before 30th May, the date they have decided signals the official start of the strawberry season.

I recently watched an episode of *That Mitchell and Webb Look* in which they performed a sketch based on Scott of the Antarctic. Oates had gone walkabout and those who remained had only a strip of dried puffin for food, which even the wasted Scott could not stomach.

'There's nothing then,' said his colleague. 'Unless...' He reaches behind him and produces, from a hamper overflowing with food, a Christmas pudding. 'The Christmas pudding,' says Scott. 'Have you gone mad? It's only August!'

My parents would have been the same. Even if they were staring starvation in the face they would not sustain themselves with a chunk of Easter egg if it was still Lent.

'Hmm... I don't like the look of your postcode'

In the days when he had a full-time job, my father would boycott the office Christmas dinner on the grounds that there was turkey on the menu and it was only the middle of December. The carpet in his living room is worn out in the spot directly in front of the drinks cabinet, as this is where he paces during the time when he is desperate for a drink but will not pour himself one as it is 'not yet six-thirty'. After Eights might have been invented for my parents: chocolates that expressly prohibit you from eating them at certain times – perfect! Forget sell-by and use-by dates. What they would really appreciate are clearly labelled 'not-to-be-eaten-before' dates.

The season for strawberry debacles is now past: tangerines are allowed, chestnuts are on sale in the local farmers' market, and my phone is ringing.

It is my mother.

'Can you look up something on your computer for me?' She always gets straight to the point – partly because she is a direct person, but also because she likes to keep the cost of phone calls down. She wants me to surf the net on her behalf because both she and my father are computer illiterate.

'I need to get hold of some cranberry liqueur,' she tells me. 'They don't sell it in the village. Can you find out where we can get some?'

'Now?' I ask. It is 9.30 in the morning, a good nine hours before official drinking time begins but, more to the point, I am trying to work.

'Yes,' she says. 'As soon as possible. We can't find any anywhere.'

'What do you need it for?' I ask, envisaging a pre-Christmas drinks party in the next few days.

'To drink,' she says. This might have been reason enough, but there is a qualifier: 'There's going to be a frost at the weekend. The first in December.'

This, I suspect, signals the official start of the cranberry liqueur-drinking season. Don't ask me why.

Renaissance on a Train

The title for **JANE GARDAM**'s *latest novel was inspired by an old wooden carving she had seen forty years previously in The Hague. But when she tried to track it down, it was as if it had never existed...*

Illustrated by **PETER BAILEY**

I have a strange tale. Last year I published my tenth novel, *The Man in the Wooden Hat*. I had wanted to call it something else – *Fidelity*, for example, or *Memory and Desire* – but was persuaded that *Fidelity* was weak and that *Memory and Desire* was a famous psycho-analytical work already. We called it *The Man in the Wooden Hat* because there is a pivotal point in my story about a lifetime's infatuation (or love perhaps) when my two old and indecisive lovers meet and part. They do this in an art gallery, the Mauritshuis, in The Hague, home of Vermeer's *Girl with a Pearl Earring* and *View of Delft*.

I had been to the Mauritshuis only once, in 1968. I was alone, and, walking from the Vermeer room into a sunny gallery, saw across one corner, I think on a plinth, a carving of the head and shoulders of a man wearing a black oak hat with an enormous brim – I guessed bog oak, perhaps seventeenth-century.

The face was holy. The eyes looked down, the mouth was gentle and the whole thing gave off peace, wisdom, godliness. I walked all round it and wanted to find out if the hat had been carved separately and set upon the head or had been carved all in one, which would have been quite a feat. I went behind the carving and tried to lift off the hat – immensely heavy. I panicked, the hat wobbled and I dropped it back, heart madly beating. I seem to remember that the figure presided over a gallery full, not of paintings, but of huge, black, carved pieces of furniture. This may be false memory. I don't know. But there was a sense of familiarity. At home when I was a child we possessed one of these ancient Nederlandisch carved armoires. My grandfather, a merchant captain, had bought it in Antwerp when my mother was a child, and carried it home on his coal-boat to Teesside. I adored it and made little campsites in its lower cupboards. It was, I was told, 'Renaissance', but my grandmother could never remember the word except that it meant 'something to do with being born again', and so we called it Nicodemus.

Well, forty years went by and I needed a site and an image of power and 'might' and love for my two old folk who had met again at The Hague, so I gave the two of them the oak man, and over it they parted for ever I thought it was quite successful.

But just as my editor and I had decided the proofs were ready for the printer to press the button, I lost confidence. Had I really seen this image at that gallery? It was obviously something very famous, set there just around the corner from the Vermeers. Suppose I'd really seen it in another gallery? Gallery-goers the world over would be after me with bricks. It is bad enough in a novel when you put someone on the wrong train. I thought I'd better check.

So I wrote to the curator of the Mauritshuis at The Hague and received a message back that there was no such exhibit in his museum and never had been in all his years in charge, but he was most interested. I thought – ah! It must have been in some other gallery we visited that summer: Leyden or Delft or Amsterdam or Bruges. But always I had the same reply.

My publisher then began a search of galleries further afield – in Italy and France. I'd have tried Spain but I have only been once to Spain, quite recently. I asked for help from two art historians and one very knowledgeable amateur. Nothing.

So I lost confidence and moved poor old Betty and Terry to another nameless gallery 'near The Hague', a gallery full of flower paintings, and it weakened the book. Terry would never have bothered to go out of the city to look at flower paintings. However – the scene took place.

A large pale man put my case on the rack. His eyes were huge, flat, blue and remote, like the dog in the fairy tale 'The Tinder Box'. He stared over my head and said 'I am Dutch. I live in The Hague...'

And was almost completely ignored when the book was published! One critic (in the *Spectator*) must have turned over two pages together because he was mystified by this man in the wooden hat. He had noticed someone wearing a felt hat from Lock's of St James in the second chapter, but why did I call it wood? He went even so far as to ring up Lock's of St James (he said in his review) to see if they had ever made wooden hats, and they said no; I'd guess in no uncertain terms.

But hats or no hats, the reviews were good and gratifying beyond belief, and the American edition in particular met with approval. I was invited to be interviewed by the influential *Publishers Weekly*, the periodical that the booksellers read. Would I go up to London from East Kent, and the journalist would come down from Oxford? We would meet at my literary agent's office in Piccadilly.

I have to say it was an effort. It was foul weather and I am eighty (as the reviews keep telling the world). But I knew that the journalist hated trains (he had nearly lost his life in the Paddington train disaster) and to Sandwich from Oxford is a slow journey in a car. I decided to drive a bit of the way to London, park my car in Canterbury overnight in the disabled car-park (I smashed my ankle in the Lake District a year or so ago) and return the next day. As I locked up the car I saw a London train coming in. It was the one before the one I'd meant to travel on, but I ran for it as you do when a train is coming, and three fat girls eating burgers all ran with me, one of them seizing my suitcase. We rushed through the tunnel under the line, and up the other side, me lolloping along behind on the ankle and shouting, 'Don't go off with it!'

When I reached the platform they were all laughing and holding the doors for me, the case already standing inside the train. I sprang in after it and the doors closed. A large pale man now took the case and put it on the rack above his head. It would have seemed rude not to have sat down opposite him at his table. Thank goodness he didn't look loquacious.

He was wearing jeans and a purple T-shirt covered in Spanish phrases. His eyes were huge, flat, blue and remote, like the dog in the fairy tale 'The Tinder Box'. He stared over my head and said, 'I am Dutch. I live in The Hague.'

There was a copy of my novel on the table. I had been going to make some notes.

'The Hague,' I said.

'In Holland.'

'Yes,' I said. 'I wonder if you go to galleries?'

'Never.'

'Not even to the Mauritshuis?'

'The Mauritshuis is not a gallery. A gallery is commercial. The Mauritshuis is a museum.'

'I suppose,' I said, 'you have never seen a carved black oak bust of a man in a sort of pilgrim hat?'

'No.'

Then he said 'Why?' and I told him.

He meditated. Then he said 'I am a computer expert. I lecture on cyberspace crime. I have just lectured in Canterbury and I am on my way to Tokyo. Have you googled this exhibit?'

'Of course. And people much better at it than I am.'

He brooded.

'But have you googled in Dutch?'

I had to admit that we had not googled in Dutch.

'I will google now in Dutch,' he said and drew up on to the table a computer, silken and thin as a biscuit, thin as the wooden hat. He plugged things in behind the lid, let his fingers fan out over the keyboard like a pianist before a performance, and began to search. After about ten seconds he said, 'Ah, yes. I have him here.'

'What! You HAVE him?'

'Yes. He is St Roch, sometimes known as the patron saint of furniture-makers. He is also of course the great saint of the road to Compostela. If you walk the pilgrim road to Compostela you will have walked in his footprints. I am a rationalist however, and do not believe in saints.'

'But where is he? He is not in the Mauritshuis.'

'No. No. He is not there. He is in a small museum south of Maastricht. It seems... look' – and he turned the screen round, and there he was in his hat – 'it seems he has been there for a very long time.'

'But I saw him at The Hague. I saw his face.'

'Yes,' said this emissary. 'Yes. He was at The Hague. But only on loan for a few months in the summer of 1968.'

'Bear with me'

GRANNY ANNEXE

Virginia Ironside

There's no rebel like an old rebel. We've had longer to practise

Have you started, yet, smiling at strangers in the street? I don't know what's come over me. I guess it's the ludicrous confidence we oldies develop as we age.

When I was young, I was a petrified snail who, as my first school report put it, 'rarely comes out of her shell'. Now I'm the first to put up my hand at committees and say appalling things like 'I think I'm speaking on behalf of everyone when I say I didn't understand a word of what you've just said!' In restaurants I dare to return meals that are inedible, or even slightly cold – recently I got an entire grouse wiped off my bill because I had been served one with blackened wings and an interior so bloody that even Hugh Fearnley-Whittingstall, the great meat-lover, would have felt sick. I can tell Jehovah's Witnesses to bugger off and, if desperate for a pee, I use the disabled toilets without a qualm. If I hear people give a good talk or a lecture, I wait by the stage for them to come off so that I can congratulate them, and if I see a particularly good performance in the theatre I write to the actor afterwards congratulating them. The cheek of it.

And, yes, I smile at strangers in the street. I live in Shepherd's Bush in London, the home of the hoodie. The Christmas before last, a young man was shot dead outside my front door, but still that doesn't put me off. When I last saw a giant gangster approaching me from the notorious White City Estate at the

When I last saw a hoodie approaching me I said to myself, 'I'm jolly well going to get a smile out of him'

top of my road, I said to myself: 'I'm jolly well going to get a smile out of him if it kills me!' And sure enough, after he'd seen my wide grin and heard my cheery 'Hello! Lovely day, isn't it?', the menacing look vanished from his face and he responded, wreathed in smiles.

Of course when we're older we also have the confidence to ask for help. As a young person I'd spent my life painting ceilings, re-caning chairs, making my own picture frames, changing my own tyres, re-wiring my own lamps, hanging my own wallpaper... Once I even made my own ping-pong table out of plywood. My then husband gave me a Black & Decker for Christmas – and, for my birthday, the *Reader's Digest DIY Manual*. I was a DIY queen, forever sanding and filling, lathing and repairing.

Now, at last, I have the confidence to ask someone else to do all these things for me. It's no longer a humiliation to stand at the bottom of the stairs at a station waiting for someone to pick up my suitcase to help me to the top. It's no longer shaming to stand by my car looking helpless when I have a flat tyre, rather than getting out the jack and trying to do it myself.

We can say 'No' to things, too, without thinking up complicated excuses. When someone rings me and says, 'I wonder, could you come to hear my god-daughter playing the oboe for charity at Ely Cathedral on a Sunday in January?' I can reply: 'No, actually, I can't.' If I'm feeling really bolshy I can say: 'Well, I can, but actually I just can't face it. I'm too bloody old.' (I haven't yet got to the point – but I will – when I give that gnomic response so beloved of old ladies, which runs: 'I'd so love to come, my dear, but I can't because you see I have the electrician coming the following day.')

At our age, we're confident enough, too, to walk out of films and theatres without waiting for the interval. When you've spent forty minutes or so watching a lousy performance, there is little more pleasurable feeling than that you experience when, after struggling past dozens of people's knees and making your way blindly up a darkened aisle, you reach the fresh light outside and breathe a sigh of relief. Free at last.

The other day at a party I was even first on the floor, asking a shy young man to accompany me. Poor wretch. And I have words with mothers who tick their children off cruelly in supermarkets, and I say 'Excuse me, I think I was first' to people who barge ahead of me in the queue.

Age has, I'm afraid, made me quite intolerable.

ILLUSTRATIONS BY ARTHUR ROBINS

Uluru

OLIVER BENNETT *takes a trip Down Under and finds himself caught between a rock and a hard place...*

A month-long sabbatical offered a chance – a 'window', you might say – of a long-haul holiday for my wife, son and me. So, after crossing off various dysentery destinations, we found ourselves bound for Australia and, like so many before us, we opted for the great triumvirate known by the ocker tourist trade as 'Rock, Reef and Harbour'.

Queensland's Great Barrier Reef and the fried barramundi of Sydney done, we took the plane to Uluru, the rock formerly known as Ayer's. In the past you had to fly to Alice Springs, some 400km distant. Now, Uluru is so alluring that it has its own airport at Yulara, the resort beside the rock. It's been growing for decades, but now it's mega, a Piccadilly Circus of the outback hosting 400,000 people a year. A company called Voyages has the monopoly, offering various categories of accommodation and tour 'packages' called things like 'Desert Awakening'.

Once you de-plane, you belong to Voyages. We stayed in its cheapest option, a youth-hostel-cum-motel called Pioneer Outback. Breeze-block cabins and tropical fauna made the sleeping quarters feel like a barracks in Kenya, while the resort itself was an unpleasant mélange of pool tables, nasty bars and vending machines. Brisk gap-year types manned the tour desks with that abrasive efficiency that London pub-goers know and abhor. There was little else to do but to visit the rock – using, of course, extortionate Voyages transport.

We got up at 4.30 am to take the sunrise trip and, after a rattling drive, alighted at a viewing point, helpfully signposted 'Viewing Point'. Yes, so industrialised was the tourism process at Uluru that we had to be told where to stand to get the photo. Around us were perhaps 200 people, holding their cameras at arm's length in that curious digital-camera outstretched pose.

It's been growing for decades, but now it's mega, a Piccadilly Circus of the outback hosting 400,000 people a year

Granted, it was beautiful. The sandstone rock did change colour in barely perceptible fashion as the sun came up, a bit like the fade-lighting in a posh spa. We took our snaps and, as we'd come millions of miles to see the damn thing, we felt it worth returning for an 'interpretive' trek in the afternoon.

Back on the bus we came, and in the afternoon light the rock was certainly magnificent, the dazzling blue of the sky setting off its dusty reds just so. We walked, finding odd moments of peace in its curvaceous gullies. But there were weird notices around about how the local Aboriginal tribe needed us to behave: you couldn't climb, women couldn't go here, no ball games... Far from being a consensus forged by some deep mystical reverence, it all had the smell of committee about it.

Any misapprehension that we'd done the right thing was dashed when we returned back to Yulara for the evening's entertainment. After a dismal supper of kangaroo burger we ended up in the bar, where a musician was torturing routine karaoke songs by the likes of Simon and Garfunkel. Instead of a middle eight guitar solo, however, each song had a didgeridoo sequence, where the player suddenly picked up a long tube and started giving it the old hoomba-hoomba.

During one of these sequences we saw a squabble develop between a tight Aboriginal man and one of the workers. Beside the bar was a notice: 'The whitefella brought grog, and the community can't handle it.' We realised that not only was Yulara a rip-off, but the place was riven with political unease: a microcosm of liberal post-colonial angst, in which a toxic mixture of condescension to 'spiritual' natives combined with high commerce and an insincere deference to tradition – which might in any case be false. A dump with a geo-political twist.

PHOTOGRAPH © ASHLEY WHITWORTH - FOTOLIA.COM

High Wind in Isfahan

When **STANLEY PRICE** *was called in to do an eleventh-hour script rewrite for a film starring Anthony Quinn, little did he realise that the great man was going to throw his toys out of the pram…*

You have to change planes in Tehran to get to Isfahan. The latter, I was told, was a beautiful city and I should visit the main mosques if I had the time. It was 1978, a year before the Shah was overthrown, but I didn't know that then and nor did he. The Shah Abbas hotel in Isfahan turned out to be at least five-star. No doubt the odd secret policeman lurked in the foyer – after all it was a very repressive regime – but surely a film-script doctor hadn't too much to fear from them. Though I had heard there was government money in the film.

In those days, film rewrites were the gilt/guilt on the professional writer's gingerbread, a lucrative and sometimes stimulating break from lonely vigils with one's current opus. This particular doctoring job, however, was not the standard chore. The sick screenplay arrived at very short notice with numerous coloured pages indicating scenes already shot. I'd never before worked on a film actually in production. As re-shooting scenes would be prohibitively expensive, the freedom to rewrite would be strictly limited and had to be done on location.

'So you're the genius who's going to pull this piece together?' said Quinn. 'That's right,' I said. It was too early to come up with a better line

The script was based on *Caravans*, a novel by James Michener, the best-selling American novelist who specialised in melodramatic sagas covering vast swathes of history set in exotic cultures.

The basic plot concerned a young American woman who marries an Afghan student, goes home with him, turns native and disappears. An American consul looks for her among an assortment of native goodies and baddies, one of whom is Zulfiqar, a Baluchi warlord, played by the film's star – Anthony Quinn.

On my first night in Isfahan, the producer, Elmo Williams, took me to dinner, appropriately in an Afghan restaurant. He was a quietly-spoken American in his early sixties. Over the starters he admitted he hadn't thought about retirement till he'd started making this movie. His young

PHOTOGRAPHY COURTESY OF SNAP/REX FEATURES

Left: the mighty Quinn staying alive (with Alan Bates)

director, who had directed a very successful Western, wasn't doing so well with a Middle Eastern. He didn't get on with the cast and they didn't get on with each other. It was debilitatingly hot shooting in the desert, and his two young American stars, Jennifer O'Neill and Michael Sarrazin, vied with each other for who could go down sick most often and have a consultant flown in from Harley Street.

We'd finished the dessert before Elmo got to Anthony Quinn. He and Elmo were the same age, which was apparently all they had in common. Quinn was of Irish-Mexican extraction, a sometime boxing champion and, according to Elmo, not the easiest of men at the best of times – which these weren't. Quinn wanted the script rewritten to give Zulffiqar a proper dramatic climax.

'Couldn't he have said that when he first read the script?'

'He was too busy negotiating his fee. Actors!' Elmo sighed, and told me how he'd once worked on a couple of Disney movies. 'It was great. You got fed up with your stars, you just tore them up.'

Elmo introduced me to Quinn early next morning. He was pushing his racing bike through the courtyard of the hotel. Apparently he cycled ten miles every morning before shooting. He looked every inch a very fit, sixty-year-old ex-boxing champion. I'd probably seen him in a dozen films, but remembered him best as the life-affirming peasant guru in *Zorba the Greek*.

'So you're the genius who's going to pull this piece together?' he said.

'That's right,' I said. It was too early to come up with a better line.

Elmo and I had our script conference on the hour's drive out to the desert location. He liked what I'd thought up on the flight out, and warned me that the four competing stars would all bang my ear. I should smile but not listen too carefully. He advised a special smile for Behrouz Vossoughi, a big Iranian star who was close to the royal family. Elmo lowered his voice so the Iranian driver wouldn't hear – 'especially Princess Ashraf, the Shah's twin sister.'

In the desert it was too hot to smile while the actors, in turn, banged my ear. Behrouz Vossoughi banged it least. He was a handsome and extremely courteous man of around thirty. Later he introduced me to the best Beluga caviar and never once demanded a rewrite in exchange.

The bulk of the writing had to be done in two weeks so I didn't move far from my large desk. From it I could look across an inner courtyard to the suite opposite. One morning I saw a man in uniform standing motionless on the parapet above the suite holding a sub-machine gun. He was watching me working. Was this how they treated their script-doctors? If you'd said two weeks they made sure it was two weeks? In a panic I raced down to reception. 'There's a man with a machine gun...' The receptionist nodded. Farah Diba, the Shah's wife, was staying at the hotel for a few days. It was one of her bodyguards. 'You won't get shot if you stay in your room,' the receptionist smiled. Iranians have a great sense of humour.

'I don't die. I'm Zorba the Greek. I stand for the life-force. I influenced a generation of our boys in Vietnam'

Farah Diba moved on, and apart from the caviar and a couple of mosques there were few distractions, so I finished on time. I had written a dramatic denouement for Zulffiqar: he dies saving the strayed American maiden. Elmo and the director seemed happy with what I'd done, and we met up with the cast in Elmo's hotel suite to discuss the changes.

First, some dilatory chat and then suddenly Quinn was advancing on me, clutching the new script, face contorted with anger. I was sitting on a low sofa and he leaned over me. He spat out, 'You think this is an ending for me? To die? I never die in my films.' He thumped his fist down on the sofa by my right ear. He pulled his fist back again. I struggled to get up. If I was going to be punched by an ex-champ I would take it like a man – standing up.

Instead he waved the script in my face and launched into a diatribe that memory synopsises into 'I don't die... I'm Zorba... Zorba the Greek... I stand for the life-force... I influenced a generation of our boys in Vietnam... together we ended the war... we chose life... I don't die in movies – not for you, not for fucking anybody.' He hurled the script on the floor and stormed out. It was as good as anything he'd done since *Lawrence of Arabia*.

After a brief cooling-off period Elmo went to beard the life-force in his suite. Next morning Elmo, now looking in his late rather than early sixties, told me Quinn was adamant about not dying. They would continue shooting my rewritten scenes but, to satisfy Quinn, find a new writer for the ending. Elmo asked me if I knew an experienced screenwriter who might fly out straight away for the same money as me. Yes, I did. My friend Michael fitted the bill and had just started paying a horrendous amount of alimony.

Michael flew in and reprieved Zulffiqar so he could ride off into the sunset. The film was finished on budget if not schedule. The reviews were not exactly glowing but, happily, neither my name nor Michael's appeared on the credits. According to the *Time Out* Film Guide, 'Unfortunately, this slice of epic schlock has all the seductive power of a syphilitic camel. There is some atmospheric photography, but Zorba the Arab inevitably spoils it all with ethnic dancing of appalling jollity. No great sheiks.'

However, the film did get one Oscar nomination – for best costume design – and Michael sent me a case of good claret.

'We've been born into a surveillance society'

A knock on heaven's door

FELIX DENNIS *nearly met his maker on a Concorde flight in 1989...*

Early one morning in June 1989, I boarded the British Airways Concorde at Heathrow bound for New York. As a regular Concorde traveller, I knew the drill: reserve seat 2B and hope to be upgraded to 1B.

Alas, no upgrade. An obscenely fat opera singer and her entourage were awarded the royal box. God knows how they squeezed her massive rear into the narrow leather seat of 1A, but eventually the thing was accomplished and we took off. From the moment we were airborne, the singer began demanding food and drink. 'I 'ungry! I 'ungry!' she chanted, flapping her cellulite-dimpled arms and poking a stubby finger into her open mouth in a pantomime gesture.

Eventually, to shut her up, the stewardesses provided her with a bottle of champagne and a couple of tubs of caviar and biscuits. In seconds, these comestibles had been demolished. 'I 'ungry! I 'ungry!' she repeated, as desperate assistants broke up enormous bars of chocolate and peeled oranges to stuff into her gaping maw. As she ate with her mouth open (in order not to miss the chance of a passing refill) this was not an edifying sight. The pretty supermodel sitting next to me smiled at my discomfort. We began to chat.

And then disaster struck. With an almighty bang, the plane lurched sideways, sheering downwards. The unmistakable smell of aviation fuel filled the interior

And then disaster struck.

With an almighty bang, the plane lurched sideways, sheering downwards, wing first. The unmistakable and terrifying smell of aviation fuel filled the interior; the entire aircraft shook and shuddered like a roller-coaster car; oxygen masks dropped; stewardesses were hurled from their feet; a nearby drinks trolley crashed on its side and liquor began leaking out; hand luggage rained down from overhead compartments; the cockpit door swung open, revealing pilot, co-pilot and navigator wrestling desperately with joysticks and punching instrument panels.

Then the screaming began. Followed by vomiting and praying aloud.

Experience counts! My seatbelt was fastened and I had instantly lifted my legs from the floor to turn my body into a pivoting fulcrum; this was to avoid spilling what was probably going to be my last drink – a large gin and tonic. The pretty supermodel had not fastened her belt and had been flung across me, her head dangling in the aisle, her chest buried in my lap. She was sobbing and tearing beads from her necklace chanting 'Holy Mary, Mother of God, pray for us sinners...' The beads spilled into the aisle and rolled away from us.

I remember thinking, as I watched the opera singer projectile-vomiting

ILLUSTRATION BY MARTIN HONEYSETT

over the front bulkhead while I gulped down terror and gin in equal measure, 'This plane is built of aluminium and titanium strip. It is one of the strongest aircraft ever built. Just STRAIGHTEN HER UP, goddamn it!'

I glanced out of the far window the edge of the leading wing was glowing cherry red, its outline distorted by heat haze and (Oh, Jesus!) the wing itself was flapping. In front of me, the large-screen digital altitude counter for passengers was flickering so rapidly I could barely read it – we had already dropped from 56,000 feet to 32,000 feet. We had a minute or two to live.

Then the terrible juddering stopped and Concorde straightened to an even keel. I heard a triumphant cry from the cockpit and saw the co-pilot grinning as only the reprieved can grin. I glanced at the altimeter display: it read 19,000 feet. The only sounds now were of sobbing and the hiss of air conditioning. The plane was travelling very quietly: we had dropped from Mach 2 to below the speed of sound and were flying on two engines, not four.

I helped the supermodel back into her seat. A stewardess was still lying prone in the aisle gripping the seat struts. An American businessman rose unsteadily and walked over the stewardess, spider-legged, towards the galley. 'Sit down, sir!' she yelled at him. 'Oh, shut up, you silly bitch,' he answered conversationally 'We just nearly died and I need a drink. We all need a drink.' Without further ado, he hoisted a couple of unbroken bottles of cognac from the trolley, cast the corks on the floor, took a mighty swig himself and calmly trudged down the aisle offering drinks. One passenger gulped a measure from her cupped hands. We were badly shaken.

Eventually, order of a kind was restored. The captain spoke on the Tannoy and apologised, explaining that a computer malfunction had cut off one engine without warning. With two engines on one side functioning and only one on the other, we had spiralled out of control. 'But the aircraft is perfectly secure now,' he assured us.

And then he said the oddest thing – perhaps it was the shock talking: 'Lucky for us that we are the only supersonic commercial aircraft in the world. Which means we fly at well over 50,000 feet. If we hadn't been that high, well... quite frankly, ladies and gentlemen, right now, we'd be a submarine! Ha ha ha!' Nobody else laughed.

300 years of Dr Johnson

To mark the tricentenary of Samuel Johnson's birth in 1709, **ANDREW MARR** told *The Oldie* what the great man means to him

SHAKESPEARE is beyond time and place; Dickens thickly coated with both; but Samuel Johnson is more thoroughly English than either. His mind was synthetic, not analytic, great scrabbling arms gathering up the world and giving it order; and his best words came in talk or hurried hack-work, when keeping private demons at bay.

I used to think I didn't like him, but only Boswell, trotting along beside him, provoking him into outrageous assertions and pearls of wisdom, and then skipping off home to write them down. And it's true that Boswell's *Life* lives more vividly than most of what Johnson laboured at in his own hand. I read Johnson's letters, his Shakespeare criticism, some of *Lives of the Poets* – but the poetry, the 'Rambler' essays, even the Dictionary? Rarely, and only in fits and starts. Those over-balanced, ponderous Latinate sentences are just too much.

Dr Johnson's house in Gough Square illustration by Peter Bailey'

I've come to understand that they too are part of his great project to hold down and give meaning to chaos. In so many of his sentences he is so alarmingly right. 'Men of the pen have seldom any great skill in conquering kingdoms, but they have strong inclination to give advice.' Let each columnist read and squirm. Or what about this? 'Almost every man's thoughts, while they are general, are right; and most hearts are pure while temptation is away. It is easy to awaken generous sentiments in privacy; to despise death when there is no danger; to glow with benevolence when there is nothing to be given.' Never better said, yet it's just the quiet background churning of an astonishing mind, the Johnson screw ticking over.

Johnson remains more of a presence than any other writer I can think of – John Bull's intelligent doppelgänger, the alarming uncle we've dreamt about but never actually encountered, the Ur-parent showering judgements and unexpected kindness, shambling and embarrassing but always better than ourselves. He's a moralist always, but a bedevilled, self-disgusted moralist, the only kind worth listening to.

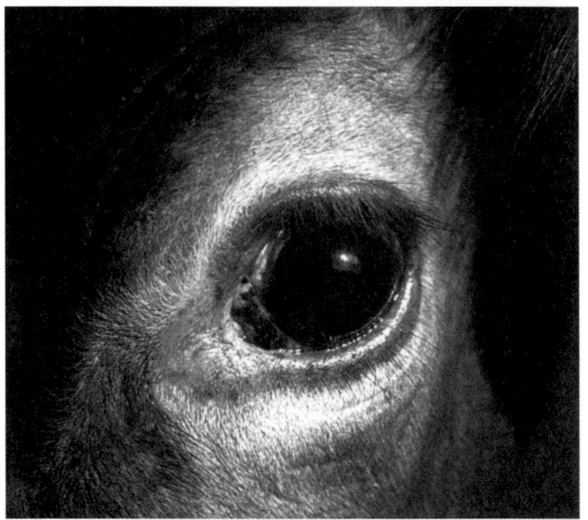

A hack with a knack

Self-effacing and reserved, the distinguished photographer **JANE BOWN** prefers not to give interviews – but after sixty years at the *Observer* and seventeen on *The Oldie* she agreed to talk to **JOHN McEWEN** about her life and work

Far left: self-portrait, 2006
Left: William Trevor, 1981 (top); cow's eye, Dartmoor, 1947 (centre); Martha Gellhorn (bottom)

Jane Bown is petite, young in style and spirit, and apt to give a question silent consideration: 'I do think words are very dangerous things.' She also once said: 'Photographers should neither be seen nor heard,' and agreed to a rare interview only out of admiration for *The Oldie*'s editor.

It was an appropriate moment: 2009 marked her sixtieth year as a photographer with the *Observer*. To celebrate the jubilee her archivist, Luke Dodd, compiled and introduced an extremely handsome book, *Exposures*, mostly of previously unseen photographs.

She lives in a house once owned by Jane Austen's brother, which she and her late husband, Martin Moss, wartime fighter pilot and a prime mover in the revival of postwar retail fashion, bought in 1954. She has three children and has always contrived to balance country and London life as adeptly as family and professional commitments permit, rarely being away for more than three mid-week days.

Her own childhood was in Dorset. 'I'm a country girl brought up by aunts: Primrose, Violet, Daisy, Iris and Ivy – a bouquet of flowers.' Her parents lived separate lives and she was an only child, so the war meant freedom. She joined the Women's Royal Naval Reserve (Wrens) and '*loved* it'. On demob she was at a loss. It was a friend who suggested she study photography. The only art college with a course was Guildford, and although photography was not then considered women's work, Ifor Thomas, ex-RNVR and head of the department, approved of a Wren.

Initially it seemed a mistake: 'All that business with lights and things, I just couldn't do it.' Then Aunt Iris gave her £50 and she bought a second-hand Rolleiflex: 'My eyes were opened – I'd found a camera I wanted to take pictures with.' The speed it encouraged suited her temperament: 'I'm a Pisces – instinctive, intuitive – all these things Pisces are meant to be.'

Aunt Iris gave her £50 and she bought a second-hand Rolleiflex. 'My eyes were opened – I'd found a camera I wanted to take pictures with'

Most professional photographers go about their business as if on heavy manoeuvres. Jane Bown arrives alone, checks the light against the back of her hand, and is gone. 'On the picture desk I'd hear them say: "Send Jane. She'll only take six minutes."'

One student vacation she photographed cows' eyes. 'Ifor hadn't thought much of me but he took a second look, then. "If you get twelve marvellous pictures like this you'll go round the world," he said. What he taught me is quality, how to get a good negative. Everything's sharp – I'm very proud of that.' For most of her career she has done her own developing. 'I wasn't a very good printer, but I still love developing those films – wiping them down, hanging them up to dry, getting up in the middle of the night when they are dry.'

Thomas was the first of her 'guardian angels'. Next came Mechthild Nawiasky, who signed her for the *Observer*. 'If you can photograph a cow's eye you can do a portrait,' she said. The 22-year-old Jane's first assignment was Bertrand Russell. 'I'd never heard of him but I was terrified. I'm quite shy of people really. The more I know them the more shy I get. I don't like photographing people I know.'

The supreme guardian angel was the *Observer*'s proprietor/editor David Astor. 'We were his kindergarten. He just plucked people out. He used to say I was prophetic. He'd get people in and ask me to photograph them. Afterwards he'd say: "Ask Jane what she thought of them."'

She had no inkling Anthony Blunt was a spy when she took him deep in shadow. Or that Jayne Mansfield would be decapitated in a car crash a week after she took her tender portrait – the last of that endlessly photographed beauty. Or that Dylan Thomas would be dead within two weeks of saying 'I don't suppose I'll see you again.'

The 22-year-old Jane's first assignment was Bertrand Russell. 'I'd never heard of him but I was terrified. I'm quite shy of people really'

Her favourite of her own photographs is of a child's feet, 'Feet Through Fence'. She likes taking children best and her first shots are invariably the most successful. She knows when she has a 'jackpot' picture – 'born of disaster half the time' – as soon as she looks into the camera. A definitive case is Samuel Beckett looking like an eagle. He was angry because she had ambushed him at the stage door after he had reneged on their appointment. 'But *he* did the photograph. It wasn't me. I've often thought: "Would anyone else in that position do as good as Beckett?" No.'

She catches the 'Iron Lady' off guard, even the Queen laughing. When the Queen presented her with the CBE she asked what she did. 'I'm a hack,' was the answer.

Her photographs have denied this from the start. As her colleague the late Patrick O'Donovan wrote, her work (she always prefers 'the simplicity and directness' of black and white) is 'journalism raised to an art form'. How was it achieved? Did she have influences? No. Does she visit art galleries? 'I never go to look at anything. I never have.' Does she like anyone else's photographs? Murdo Macleod. Music? 'I have classical music on half the time but I don't really listen.' Reading? 'I used to promise myself – when I get older I'm going to read. Do I read now? No. I do the crossword. I'm lucky to have my brain.' Does age have any compensations? 'None whatsoever.' Is she a believer? 'I'm a country believer. The other day I went to the old church in Dorset I used to go to as a child. It was so lovely. It smelt just the same.'

So what is the secret? 'Honestly, it's a complete mystery to me,' she smiles. 'It's a knack. I call it a knack. With my Rolleiflex you used to suddenly see into the eyes – rather like the cow's eye – and something comes back. I do love who I'm looking at – there's a moment. People are marvellous. But I'm not a portrait photographer. Everyone thinks of me as a portrait photographer. I don't. What do I think I am? I'm a cow's eye photographer. I just like taking pictures and where I'm naughty now is I don't do it anymore. I ought to, I see pictures all the time, but I can't be bothered. I think I've shot my bolt.'

Jane Bown's countless fans will hope not, but if she has, what a bolt she has shot.

• ***Exposures*** **is published by Guardian Books, 224 pp, HB, £30**

The *strange* death of Old Labour

In 1979 the teetering Labour Government was finally brought down on a motion of no confidence. **AUSTIN MITCHELL** *remembers the machinations behind the vote*

On 28 March 1979 the post-war political era came to an end when Jim Callaghan's Government was defeated by one vote on a confidence motion brought by Margaret Thatcher. Labour lost the subsequent election and faced nearly two decades of re-grouping and transformation before it got back to power as New Labour.

Over 200 of the MPs who voted on that night are still with us, and in March 2009, on the thirtieth anniversary of the vote, fifty of them attended a reunion at the House of Lords at the invitation of Joe Ashton, then Labour MP for Bassetlaw. They were welcomed by Lord Speaker, Helene Hayman, who, as a very young Labour MP for Welwyn and Hatfield – nicknamed 'Miss Cheesecake of 1977' by the Labour lags – had participated in the vote.

The Labour Whips in 1979 were a battle-hardened team of thugs who'd bullied, bribed and cajoled to keep Labour skating long after the thin ice had melted. The key man in Labour's 'want of a nail' drama was Deputy Chief Whip Walter Harrison. As former Whip Alf Bates recalled: 'Walter never took anything for granted when we were going to have a vote – you never knew what rabbits he would pull out of the hat. But he didn't have any rabbits left by March 1979.'

Indeed, some of the rabbits were dying. Ten days before the vote, Tom Swain, ex-miner and boxer, and MP for Derbyshire North East, was killed in a road accident. The seat was safe, but there was no time to call a by-election. Another MP, Dr Alf Broughton, was dying of emphysema. Whip Ted Graham recalled: 'Doc Broughton wanted to come but Jim took the decision not to bring him down because it would kill him. Keeping the Government going wasn't worth a life. On the next day he said to his wife, "How did we get on?" She told him we'd lost. He turned his face to the wall and was dead in 24 hours.'

Labour had always relied on the Irish Nationalists, Gerry Fitt and Frank Maguire, but they both abstained. At the time we thought Maguire abstained because Gerry Fitt attacked him and Roy Mason, Northern Ireland Secretary, in the House, but Joe Ashton provided a different explanation: 'Walter was Chairman of the Security Committee, though it was kept totally secret. The IRA wanted the Tories to win the vote because they knew that Mrs Thatcher would take a much tougher line, and that would strengthen them in Northern Ireland. Walter was told that if Fitt and Maguire voted with the Government the IRA would kill them, their wives and families. He knew it could happen and it was only two days after the vote that they killed Airey Neave. Maguire and Fitt knew it too.'

The Ulster Unionists put another nail in our coffin. Roy Hattersley, who was negotiating with the Unionists, proposed offering a gas pipeline to Northern Ireland, but Jim Callaghan, wearying of the struggle and tired of press attacks on him for bullying and bribing, vetoed it. Two of the Unionists wanted special measures to bring down inflation – we got their votes but not the rest. Jim Lester, then a Tory Whip, said that afterwards they found out that Enoch Powell, then an Ulster Unionist, while reluctantly supporting the Tories, had in fact arranged with Roy Hattersley to persuade two Unionists to vote with the Government. 'He came into our lobby with a big smile because he thought he'd fixed it. When the vote was announced I watched his face. He was horrified.'

Although the Liberals wouldn't support us, it was hoped that Clement Freud could be persuaded to abstain by an offer to support his Private Member's Freedom of Information Bill. Freud was in Liverpool. Could he miss his train? He was phoned. His answer was 'No'. He came to vote, and Freedom of Information was delayed for twenty years.

The Welsh Nats (in the event only two of them) had been bought off by an offer to compensate quarry workers with lung disease – but what could we offer the Scot Nats? The devolution referendum had just taken place with a majority voting 'Yes'. However, the Yes voters comprised just over a third of the Scottish electorate, and in an amendment to the 1978 Scotland Act

PHOTOGRAPH COURTESY OF PRIVATE EYE; CARICATURE OF AUSTIN MITCHELL BY ROBERT GEARY

prompted by anti-devolution Labour MP George Cunningham, the threshold had been set at forty per cent. At the reunion, Cunningham denied responsibility for Labour's defeat: 'That Government was doomed. Even if it hadn't fallen in May it would have fallen in October.' Yet the forty per cent requirement meant that Labour now had nothing to offer to stop the SNP MPs voting with the Opposition – described at the time by Michael Foot as 'turkeys voting for Christmas' (although according to Hamish Watt, then SNP Whip, two of the 'turkeys', himself and George Reid, did want something from the Government, 'but Walter wouldn't deal with us. I couldn't understand why Walter wasn't working as hard as he usually did. He'd worked to the last second every day but on that particular day he stopped at 4 pm – I always had the feeling that Jim had decided he'd had enough and he didn't ask Walter to work as hard as he otherwise would have done.')

A conga chain of top totty and prospective Tory candidates formed in the Central Lobby and danced down the passage into the Families Room where Tory wives and families joined in

When the time came for the vote, the Whips fanned out to do their duties. Frank White and Ted Graham were 'flushers', tasked with looking under lavatory doors to see if anyone was in and jumping up and looking over to identify them. If Labour, they were hauled out – Tories were left to sleep on. Tom Cox held up a notice-board telling people how to vote. Alf Bates was sent out to the neighbouring bars, because with the Commons' catering staff on strike no food was being provided inside.

The Chamber was packed, and the immediate result unclear. Robin Corbett, then MP for Hemel Hempstead, remembered the scene: 'I heard Jimmy Hamilton, the Labour Whip, come in and say "We've won," and give the thumbs up. He was wrong. The rest is history.'

Private Eye cover, 30 March 1979

Not quite. A conga chain of top totty and prospective Tory candidates formed in the Central Lobby and danced down the passage into the Families Room where Tory wives and families joined in (Labour wives glaring) and they all danced back to the Central Lobby. Tory members went off to get the food and drink they couldn't get in the Commons. Jim Lester went with Ken Clarke to Ronny Scott's.

Labour Whips were more practical. Peter Snape recalled that 'some sympathetic Ministers told others to empty their cocktail cabinets because the civil servants will lock them tomorrow. So they brought all their booze down to the Whips' Office and we got well and truly pissed. We were there at 7.30 the next morning. It looked like Hitler's bunker in the last days of the Reich.'

I got drunk on red wine with journalist Llew Gardner and politics professor Richard Rose, who tried to persuade me that my majority of 520 would see me through. The next day we all hurried off to our constituencies to face an election which had been hanging over us for months as our prospects darkened.

It was disastrous. Some, such as Eric Moonman, then Labour MP for Basildon, are bitter, blaming it all on Jim: 'Everything he did was a mistake. It's the sort of thing that happens to Prime Ministers. Whatever documents are put in front of them about the likely chance of winning they just go on, as he did in October 1978. It was foolish. He ruined the lives of many young men and women, me included.' Others, like Arthur Davidson, are more philosophical: 'The vote didn't come as a surprise. The timing was wrong but it was time for an election... I'm not sure it would have made any difference if we'd been able to hang on.... so when it came it was a relief. The Government was very tired... I just didn't think we could win.'

We didn't. Margaret Thatcher swept to power and the demolition gang moved in on Old Labour.

Whiteboard jungle

Neither **KATE SAWYER** *nor her Year Tens are overly impressed with the sex education syllabus...*

Five women sit around a table and stare solemnly at an erect pink plastic penis. I suspect we all have the urge to giggle but we are trying hard to behave. In a way the penis is fascinating, and I watch the women trying not to look as though they are really looking at it. It's just somehow there. But it does stop conversation.

We are all about to be trained in how to deliver sex education to Year Tens. We are volunteers. I am not quite sure why. I think I envisaged gentle discussions about love and romance, perhaps with a little Elizabeth Barrett Browning thrown in. I suspect I had some mad idea about a moral crusade to stop the young becoming promiscuous or parents or both. Whatever the reason was, faced with the penis it seems mad. (A part of my brain picks that up and thinks yes, point that out to the girls. Decisions and penises...) I certainly did not think I would be teaching the biology of sex education.

And, it turns out, I'm not. That has already been covered in science lessons (Phew). I'm going to be teaching them how to put a condom on, how to check whether the condom is usable, how not to catch STIs. (And not having sex is not the answer.) It is stressed that we must make no mention of flavoured or otherwise enhanced condoms, as we are not to imply that sex is fun. The message seems to be that as everyone is doing 'it' they must be protected from the consequences, but that 'it' is a dangerous necessity rather than having any bearing on human relations.

ILLUSTRATED BY PETER BAILEY

When I see what is nestled inside I lose my self-control and an unladylike and unteacherly snort escapes me

The nurse who is training us then produces a Powerpoint presentation showing hideously diseased genitalia. The five of us, who had just begun nervously tittering as the condoms were rolled out, are struck dumb at the pictures. I am sure they will mentally scar the young, and wonder if I too am not mentally scarred.

Out of another box comes a plastic breast with secret hidden lumps in it, and the equivalent testicular toy. We all squeeze and prod and find the hidden cancers with a certain amount of unholy glee. After all, it is only plastic.

When the day comes I reach for my box of condoms and penises with some trepidation. It is only when I open it and I see what is nestled inside that I finally lose my self-control and an unladylike and unteacherly snort escapes me. For the penis they have given me for the lesson is not so much bright pink, nor a politically correct shade of brown, but is bright blue. What, I wonder, is the message implied there?

The next day I ask the Year Tens what they thought of the lesson. A girl looks at me thoughtfully. 'Well, Miss, they've been showing us how to put condoms on for years. They've been telling us about pregnancy and STIs for ever. I just wish someone would talk to us about the emotional side of sex. They never give us any help there.'

How shall I love thee? Let me count the ways... I knew a bit of love poetry would have been a good idea.

'He's tunnelled out!'

BORE TV (See Digital Channel 356)

This week's highlights 4 – 10 January 2010

✤ MASTERCHEF: SPECIAL DIETARY REQUIREMENTS

Monday 6:45pm, Bore TV

It's the semi-final stage, and things are really hotting up. The contestants face a tough vegan breakfast. And how will they cope cooking for a wheat-intolerant wedding? (S) (146142)

✤ BACK TO THE STONE AGE

Tuesday 9pm, Bore TV

Maurice Thong is in the Forest of Compiègne seeking out the herbs which our remote ancestors probably used as aphrodisiacs. And grilled mole turns out to be a tasty dish when combined with a sauce made from finely ground bluebell bulbs. (S) (847339)

✤ OBESITY FILE

Friday 8pm, Bore TV

Dr Ahmed Sharif visits Clare, an 11-year-old Birmingham schoolgirl so fat she is unable to get out of bed. Dietician Christine Onanugu is in San Diego talking to worshippers at the USA's first church for obese Christians. (S) (822246)

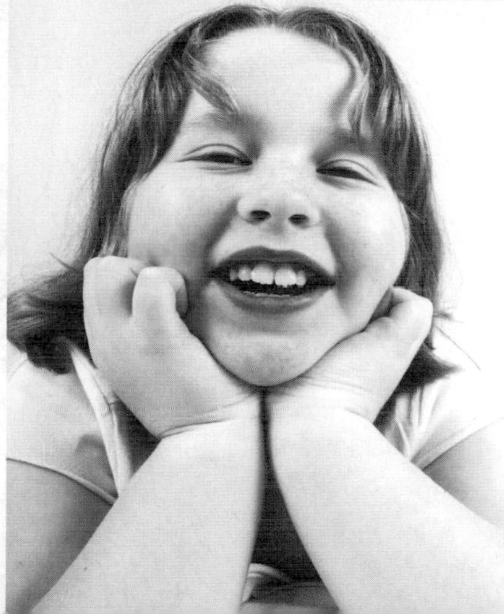

✤ A NIGHT AT THE HOT DOGS

Wednesday 11:30pm, Bore TV

The hunt is on to find the best hot dog stand in Lancashire. Mariella Stothard tracks down two of the finalists, Alfredo Barcarolle and Boris Mangold. Now it's up to the judges, headed by Prue Leith, to pronounce their verdict. (S) (629114)

✤ SCRAPYARD SHOWDOWN

Friday 9:30pm, Bore TV

The He-Men of Huddersfield meet the Chorleywood Crazies in the grand finale of this year's series. Both four-man teams must make a helicopter solely from material found in the massive Solihull scrapyard. Cindy Lavage presents. (S) (124233)

✤ THE WORLD'S DEADLIEST MOTHS

Friday 8pm, Bore TV

Shane Faulkner travels to Tierra del Fuego in search of the deadly Mexican Vampire Moth and talks to expat Barry Tisdall, whose leg was amputated after a bite from the so-called 'Angel of Death'. (S) (777211)

✤ DECISION

NEW SERIES

Friday 8:30pm, Bore TV

As Christmas approaches, single mum Rhiannon has a crucial decision to make. Her parents have recently split and both of them want her to be with them on Christmas Day. Her mother Becky has moved to Swansea and it's a long drive from Darlington with two small children. But her father is an alcoholic and is now living with another man. What will her devoted social-worker friend Maddy advise? (S) (141142)

PICK OF THE WEEK

✤ PLINTHWATCH, LIVE

Monday 7:30pm, Bore TV

Live footage from the fourth plinth of Trafalgar Square. This week: will the engineers fix the persistent fault with the hydraulic crane? (S) (222772)

A double suicide in Tokyo ....

Best feet forward

JAMES KIRKUP *invites us to take our first faltering steps into the complex world of Japanese shoe etiquette...*

Japanese society is one in which most people seek every occasion to take off their shoes. The very act of entering a house is an illustration of this. Whenever a Japanese front door opens to our gaze, we behold a strange assortment of footwear, from babies' bootees to day labourers' very short gumboots. Every time you enter a Japanese house you are requested to remove your footwear.

Space is limited, so anyone who arrives in a pair of bucket-topped buccaneer swashbuckling thigh-boots is accorded particular respect and attention. Those who imagine they are being clever by wearing easily-slipped-off moccasins or loafers will receive no more than minimal consideration. It is advisable to take along a few plastic clothes pegs, preferably of varying pastel shades, to clip on to the tops of your thigh-length boots, in order to retain your body warmth and your own precious foot aromas.

Once inside the 'mansion' or 'demeure' or 'heights' or 'haus' – the Japanese hate to use their own language, preferring bastard foreign terms – you will discover that there are many opportunities for you to remove and put on various kinds of footwear. As soon as you step up from the *genkan* or *horu* (hall) onto the highly polished wooden boards of the diminutive passage, you will be pressed to insert your already-cooling summer feet into house slippers with thick felt soles and adorned with pretty pompoms. These may be worn in the Western-style living room, with carpets, pianos, tables and armchairs all draped in heavy, crocheted antimacassars.

On entering the traditional Japanese room with *tatami* mats, you will be obliged to remove your house slippers at the sacred threshold, and be careful to leave them pointing outwards, so that you may step into them the more gracefully on leaving the room.

The best way to remove your house slippers on passing from wooden floor to *tatami* floor is to enter the room backwards, with a slight bow, to avoid braining yourself on the low fretwork lintel which, if you do happen to knock it, will shower you with a decade of snuff-like dust.

But there is more footwork to come. After kneeling for the prescribed five and a half minutes before the *tokonoma* to admire hissingly the works of art there enshrined – a long scroll consisting mainly of mist in various shades of grey and a poem calligraphed with masterly hand, and tendrils of withered wisteria hanging from the top of this yellowed

oblong of paper fixed to a brocade backing; together with a pot containing untranslatable flowers, leaves and scraps of flotam and jetsam – you hope to be able to relieve the pressure on your knee-caps which have seized up as if they will never again unseize. Hauling yourself to your aching feet you find you are being invited (with many a bow and ushering movements of the right hand) to step onto the balcony to enjoy the scintillating view – towering apartment blocks lit stem to stern like ocean-going liners, and a distant red neon sign. But before you can tread the well-swept concrete or wooden floor of this airy extension of the living quarters, you have to encase your feet in special balcony clogs that go clink-clunk with a kind of death-rattle.

After duly admiring, with gasps of unfeigned astonishment, the nocturnal urban scene, comes the tricky moment when you must re-enter the formal Japanese living-room. This involves creeping crab-like on your wooden balcony clogs – your heels hanging well over the backs, and your toes barely able to insert themselves into the plastic overstrap – until you have your back to the sliding window. Then you neatly slide your stockinged feet out of the confining clogs and enter the lamplit chamber backwards, slipping your mortified feet into those capacious house-slippers, toes dutifully turned towards the balcony, as is only right and proper.

After a decent interval your host may, by some inscrutable means, insinuate that you might like to explore the geography of his home. You must never be so crudely American as to request 'May I use your bathroom?' If you do, your host will assume that you wish to take a bath. Instead, just sit and wait, and in the end you will somehow be conducted to the Japanese toilet or *benjo*, with its musical toilet roll playing the first inspiriting bars of 'Sobre las Olas'. Out of consideration for your modesty, the host will turn up the radio, letting the NHK 'My Home Symphony' programme cover any unseemly blast or brook-like babblings.

In order to enter the very circumscribed toilet you must exchange your cosy house slippers for yet another special pair of dwarf clogs that allow you to proceed only on tiptoe. Here you may leave your house slippers pointing towards the glass-panelled portal, the better to negotiate the tricky transfer of your outsized trotters to the tottery baby-blue plastic clogs. On emerging from the toilet, having flushed it once, then swirled its deodorant waters with a plastic toilet-bowl brush with rainbow nylon bristles, then flushed it again, you step backwards into the reassuring comfort of the house slippers, waiting demurely outside the door, where a hot towel or *oshibori* is steaming for you in a wee wicker basket woven with a few silk roses. Your host switches off the NHK pandemonium, a sign that you may return to the civilised amenities of the Japanese living-room.

In my opinion the high level of suicides among the Japanese comes from this yearning to remove their shoes at each and every opportunity. This is because Japanese shoemakers do not know how to make comfy shoes, and Western-made ones do not suit the metatarsal uniqueness of the Japanese foot – so the Japanese always appear to be hobbling like Mrs Thatcher with corns. They are forever muttering, silently, 'my feet are killing me', and take every opportunity to throw off those torturing toe-crushers, dropping them at temples, shrines and bathhouses.

Every foolish, idol-crazed Japanese teenage girl who throws herself off the fifteenth-floor balcony first removes her shoes. Every bankrupt sharpster atones for his commercial ineptitude by jumping in front of a subway train – after first neatly arranging his crippling shoes on the edge of the platform, toes pointing towards the rails. Sometimes, on an express train, I see a pair of abandoned boots pointing towards the door, and I know that some Japanese shoe-fetishist has taken the supreme step and cast himself off a speeding train, for the simple pleasure of relieving his martyred feet. Such is the be-all and end-all of this uniquely Japanese obsession of finding excuses at every turn of their daily lives – and, I suspect, in their most pedestrian dreams – to remove their footwear.

If you want to step onto the balcony you must first encase your feet in special balcony clogs that go clink-clunk with a kind of death-rattle

RANT

PASSING the British Museum recently, I decided to pop in for a dash of the sublime. What a shock. Tickets for the Hadrian exhibition had sold out, and when I tried to visit the Reading Room it was shut – because the Hadrian exhibition was in there. I asked when it would be open again and was told 'Perhaps in 2012'.

It transpires that this iconic heart of the British Museum, recently restored at public expense and the grand climax of Foster's magnificent reconstruction of the Great Court, has been 'taken out', hidden and refitted as exhibition space. Why? Because so much exhibition space has been handed over to shops and cafés.

As a restorative, I thought to visit the basement galleries of Greek and Roman sculpture. They were closed. I've been trying to visit them for ten years. They are always closed. I should say 'revisit' because I remember them from my youth as being packed with wonders. Enough disappointment for one day – on my way out I passed the huge main staircase which was also closed for no reason that anyone could explain. I suspect it is to force everyone through the Great Court and more shops.

The British Museum is one of our top tourist attractions but the experience was of a messy, crowded shopping arcade with some galleries and cafés attached. I can think of no greater advertisement for the educational incompetence and abject philistinism of the current British state.

I made these points in a letter to the *Times*. A man called Roy Clare, 'Chief Executive, Museums, Libraries and Archives Council', replied to the effect that since Hadrian was a sell-out, no one has cause for complaint. To believe that the Museum's core purpose is to sell out temporary, commercial shows reveals a terrible malaise. Does Egypt want its mummies back?

DUNCAN FALLOWELL

ILLUSTRATION BY TOM PLANT

Decline
of the English robbery

DUNCAN CAMPBELL examines a half-century of villains, thugs and cunning plans – and finds that even crooks aren't quite what they used to be...

It was called the Great Mailbag Robbery and took place more than half a century ago, just north of Oxford Circus. One of the reports at the time suggested that it was carried out with 'Montgomery-like thoroughness... It went off as smoothly as any of our commando raids during the war.' A mail van on its way from Paddington Station to St Martin's-le-Grand General Post Office yard was boxed in on Eastcastle Street by a black Riley and a green Vauxhall while the robbers helped themselves to £287,000 – no mean sum in 1952. The culprits were, suggested the *Daily Mirror*, 'probably ex-Borstal boys, expert motor drivers'.

Roll on to 2006 and south to Tonbridge in Kent, where the biggest robbery ever carried out in Britain took place. No Rileys and Vauxhalls this time, but a certain military precision as £53 million is removed from the Securitas depot by a team of robbers. The manager, his wife and young son are kidnapped at gunpoint and held until the money has been stolen by men dressed as police officers and disguised by latex masks. In October 2009, the last of the gang in British custody, Paul Allen, was jailed for 18 years, joining five of his associates already behind bars. Most of the dosh is still missing.

The 1952 mailbag job caused political ructions that led to the Postmaster General, Earl de la Warr, having to explain himself to Parliament. The Prime Minister, Winston Churchill, asked for daily reports of the investigation from Detective Chief Superintendent Bill 'Cherub' Chapman, but the Tonbridge job never acquired the same cachet. It represents, in many ways, the decline of the English robbery.

The fact that both Allen and his friend, Lee Murray, the alleged ringleader currently in jail in Morocco, were both steroid-using cage fighters was the Tonbridge robbery's most distinguishing feature. There were no pumped-up cage fighters in the business fifty years ago, but big set-piece robberies have changed in many other ways. The 1952 grab in Eastcastle Street resulted in no convictions, although it was well known to have been organised by the late Billy Hill, a man who, a few years later, launched his ghosted autobiography, *Boss of Britain's Underworld*, at Gennaro's in Soho, now the site of the Groucho Club. Arrests on the Tonbridge robbery, by contrast, followed almost before the robbers had had time to park their getaway lorry, a sign that the planning had been more impulsive.

The mailbag job was itself superseded in criminal lore, of course, by the 1963 Great Train Robbery. That was master-

Back right: 1952 mailbag job mastermind Billy Hill, with his mob

PHOTOGRAPHY COURTESY OF: GRAHAM JEPSON AND POPPERFOTO/HUTON ARCHIVE/GETTY IMAGES

minded by Bruce Reynolds, a jazz-loving existentialist and admirer of the writing of Jean Genet. Reynolds, in his autobiography, suggests that he was searching for his 'Eldorado – more for the adventure than the financial rewards'. When finally caught by Detective Chief Superintendent Tommy Butler, he remarked: 'C'est la vie, Tom.'

Most, but not all, of the train robbers were caught and given 30-year jail sentences. One of them, Ronnie Biggs, has only just been released, after a couple of gap decades in Brazil.

The most spectacular robbery in the Seventies was probably the 1971 Baker Street bank robbery, which had the virtue that no one was injured or threatened. Remarkably, a young radio ham picked up conversations between the robbers while it was actually happening. Their weary look-out man was giving them

Police at the scene after the 1963 Great Train Robbery

Police enter Lloyds Bank in Baker Street following the robbery in 1971

a running commentary on his walkie-talkie from a vantage point on the roof opposite as they tunnelled into the bank from a neighbouring handbag shop. The ham alerted the police, who duly found the bank's door locked – it was the weekend, so there were no staff around – and left. No one realised what had happened till staff entered the vaults the following Monday.

That robbery inspired the recent film, *The Bank Job*, starring Jason Statham and Saffron Burrows. Its promotional material suggested that 'none of the money was ever recovered, nobody was ever arrested... the robbery made headlines for a few days and then disappeared – the result of a government D-Notice gagging the press.' This is all nonsense, although it has been trustingly repeated in reviews by some of our most distinguished film critics. In fact, four men were caught and jailed for a total of 48 years, more than £250,000 was recovered, no D-Notice was ever issued and the case was widely reported.

A radio ham picked up conversations between the robbers while it was actually happening. He alerted the police, who duly found the door locked ... and left

As is often the case, the factoid is more entertaining than the facts. The film, which came out in 2008, also shows evidence of other cultural changes. The original ending in the 1960 Basil Dearden film, *The League of Gentlemen*, starring Jack Hawkins and Richard Attenborough, had the (fictional) ex-army robbers getting away with their crime. But this was seen to be sending the wrong message, so the script was changed and they all ended up in a Black Maria; crime could not be seen to pay. No such morally improving endings are required today in crime films, whether fictional or factual.

By the Eighties, too, robbers were more violent. The gang who stole gold bullion from the Brinks Mat depot at Heathrow in 1983 poured petrol over a security guard and threatened to set fire to him.

And so to Tonbridge. What made it so different from the earlier crimes was the decision to kidnap a woman and child, not something of which the old school approved. Then there was the involvement of two Albanians, one of whom, a former employee, was an inside man; previously such an operation would have been purely domestic, carried out by people who knew each other well. Latex masks, those disguises that actors now regularly peel off their faces in spy films, represent a technological shift from the ski mask, which had itself replaced the balaclava and the stocking mask.

Still, it all has to be seen in context. A year ago I bumped into someone whose robbery trial I had covered years earlier at the Old Bailey; he had been acquitted then, thanks to a cock-up made by a couple of greedy, bribe-seeking detectives, and he had since managed to send his sons to good public schools. They were all now working in the City. If only he had known, he said, how easy it was to help yourself to cash that way, he would never have wasted his time taking risks and going to jail. Now that we can see that the best-rewarded rogues in Britain are the ones who wear ski masks only to ski and carry guns only to shoot slow-moving game birds, we must remind ourselves of Bertolt Brecht's maxim: 'What is the crime of robbing a bank compared with the crime of founding one?'

• Duncan Campbell's gangster novel *If It Bleeds* is published by Headline, £7.99. Billy Hill's book *Boss of Britain's Underworld* is available from the website run by his son, Justin. See www.billyhill.co.uk for more details.

Voice from the Grave

'Our finances have been brought into grave disorder. No British Government in peace-time has ever had the power or spent the money in the vast extent and reckless manner of our current rulers... No community living in a world of rapidly competing nations can possibly afford such frantic extravagances... the evils which we suffer today are inevitable progeny of that wanton way of living.'
Winston Churchill in the *Conservative Party Manifesto for the General Election of 1951*

Robert GEARY

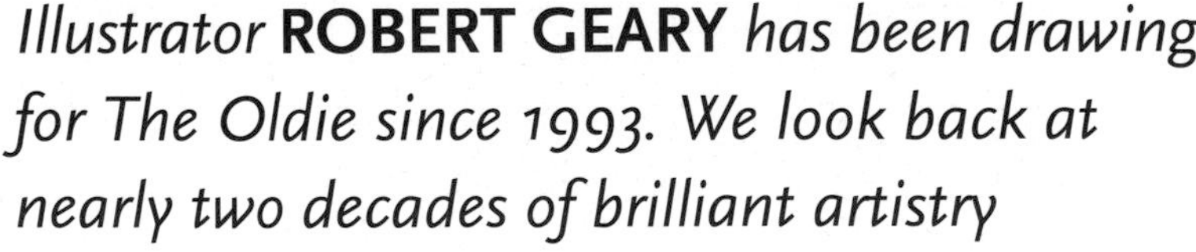

Illustrator **ROBERT GEARY** *has been drawing for The Oldie since 1993. We look back at nearly two decades of brilliant artistry*

THIS PAGE, CLOCKWISE FROM ABOVE: self-portrait reading *The Oldie*; V S Naipaul; Sybil Thorndike as Shaw's St Joan
FACING PAGE, TOP ROW (l–r): Louis Armstrong; Martin Amis
MIDDLE ROW (l–r): Cardinal Basil Hume; Alan Bennett
BOTTOM ROW (l–r): John Mortimer; David Sutch, aka Screaming Lord Sutch

VOTE LORD SUTCH
VOTE LORD
I BET I WILLBEAT WILLIAM HILL

Wilfred Lawson on the set of the 1954 film *Make Me an Offer*

Wilfred Lawson

PATRICK GARLAND *recalls one of the great characters – both on and off the stage*

It is difficult to describe what Wilfred Lawson looked like – it was more important to hear the way he spoke. There was a time in the Fifties and Sixties when, along with John Gielgud and Robert Atkins, Wilfred Lawson was one of the three most imitated actors in Britain. He had a very recognisable, eccentric manner of speech, somewhat whining, with exaggeratedly sibilant consonants. He gave a mesmerising performance of the Old Man in Gorki's *The Lower Depths* at the Arts Theatre, and I remember seeing an overawed Laurence Olivier wandering about Leicester Square afterwards with a glazed expression on his face.

Wilfred Lawson was a magnetic and compelling actor when he wasn't drunk, which he frequently was – a character man, not in any sense a leading man, but a completely authentic performer. He appeared in *The Lower Depths* with my old friend Bryan Pringle who told me that Wilfred was spontaneous with the lines and was liable to go into extraordinary and unexpected improvisations. 'We're all born men,' he was supposed to say, 'and we all die men. It's the whole giddy blasphemy of life.' He sometimes found this line very difficult to remember

A member of the audience heckled: 'You're pissed.' Without batting an eyelid, Wilfred replied, 'You think I'm pissed, wait till you see the Duke of Buckingham'

accurately, and made lively variations on it, such as, 'We're all born men and we all die men. It's the whole giddy who-ha-ha-ha of life.' On another occasion he said to Pringle, 'We are all born men and we all die men. It's the whole giddy... What do you think it is?'

When he was leaving the stage, Bryan would call out to him, 'Goodbye, old man,' and Wilfred would reply 'Goodbye,' and walk a little further off stage. 'Goodbye, old man,' Bryan would shout again, and Wilfred would turn at the edge of the stage and say 'Goodbye' again. When he was almost completely off stage, Bryan would call out a final time, 'Goodbye, old man.' Wilfred would turn at the edge of the scene, half in the shadows and, addressing the audience, say, 'Will someone tell him to piss off?'

Wilfred was also famous for some

PHOTOGRAPH COURTESY OF POPPERFOTO/GETTY IMAGES

film roles. Before the war he was a definitive Alfred Doolittle in the film of Shaw's *Pygmalion*, earning the whole-hearted admiration of Rex Harrison, a man notoriously difficult to please, who thought Wilfred one of the finest character actors of the age. And in 1955, he was remarkable in the part of the prison guard in the film version of *The Prisoner*, starring Alec Guinness.

'Allowed to roam free? This chicken's had a better life than me!'

Nigel Stock once told me that he was very disconcerted by being on stage with Wilfred: 'The trouble with Wilfred was you never knew what he was going to say next, if you were lucky enough for him to say anything at all; he often made up the lines as he went along, but of course it did give him this great gift of spontaneity.' Nigel appeared with him in *The Father*, one of Wilfred's most famous roles. It had one of those Strindbergian opening scenes and Wilfred was liable to say whatever occurred to him. At the end of it, Nigel, playing the part of the family doctor, had to say in some exasperation to Wilfred, 'Well, all I can say, sir, is that I wash my hands of the whole affair.' He was about to make his exit, but before he could reach the door, Wilfred turned to the audience and casually said, 'You can wash your cock if you like.'

I remember seeing Wilfred in the tiny but electrifying role of the button-moulder in a production of *Peer Gynt* at the Old Vic – though on that occasion his performance was not enhanced by his announcing, when he appeared at the corner of the stage, 'I'm a mutton boulder'. He once appeared with his friend Trevor Howard in a production of *Richard III*. Trevor played the Duke of Buckingham, and Wilfred played the King. When he came on, a member of the audience, noticing the state he was in, heckled loudly, shouting, 'You're pissed.' Without batting an eyelid or dropping a pentameter, Wilfred replied, 'You think I'm pissed, wait until you see the Duke of Buckingham.' But sometimes he was unfairly judged since he always seemed drunk whether he was or not.

There was a famous occasion when Peter O'Toole and Richard Burton, who were making a film together, visited Wilfred when he was appearing in a touring play nearby. They drank until the early hours but Burton and O'Toole had to give up because they had a prompt call at 4 am to resume filming. 'That's the trouble with the youth of today; they've got no stamina,' Wilfred complained. 'When Trevor Howard and I and Boney Crawford were filming in the war, we used to drink all day long and put on our make-up on the way to Elstree Studios on the Tube at 5 am.'

It was never wise to rehearse with Wilfred in the afternoon, as he generally retired to the pub for lunch, but no one could deny his marvellous ability: he was always a remarkably instinctive actor and frequently a very conscientious one.

One of the last occasions I saw Wilfred was in a play at the Royal Court. In one scene, he and Bryan Pringle had to be locked in a cupboard together. The stage management decided to lock them in the cupboard, and gave them a crate of Guinness to keep them entertained while the play went on. From the cupboard one could hear the clatter of bottle tops dropping on the floor, the clink of glass, suppressed belching and the fizzing noises of bottled beer being poured out.

On another occasion Wilfred met Peter O'Toole in the pub near the Royal Court at Sloane Square, and after they had drank several bottles of Guinness, they decided to retire to the gallery of the theatre to carry on their conversation. They went upstairs with a couple of bottles of Guinness only to discover that the play was already in progress. They stayed at the back of the gallery, whispering to each other and drinking their Guinness and occasionally looking at the play. All of a sudden Wilfred nudged O'Toole in the ribs. 'This is a good bit,' he said. 'I come on here...!'

Crying Wolf

BEN MALLALIEU *braved freezing temperatures in Poland for a glimpse of a wolf*

I am sitting in a high seat in a dark East European forest in the snow, and I am waiting for the wolves, and very cold it is too. These words are forming like snowflakes in my head largely because there is not a lot else to do. It's like being in a flotation tank with the heating turned off, or one of those cells where Tibetan monks are walled up for years on end. Sometimes you think you notice odd sounds in the wind or shapes in the shadows, but mostly you are aware of nothing except your brain drifting off at tangents.

And 'high seat' is a somewhat misleading term, implying the kind of chair that tennis umpires sit in. In fact, it's a rudimentary wooden box on stilts, with no mod cons other than a bucket to pee in and a wooden plank to sit on. This one looks out onto a clearing known, perhaps a little optimistically, as the Wolf Meadow, with a narrow stream meandering noisily through the middle.

When I told a wildlife photographer I was going to Poland to see wolves, he looked at me pityingly. 'Go to Alaska,' he said. But I'm not really bothered about seeing actual wolves close to – they are only dogs with attitude. It's the idea of wolves that's so potent – the heart-chilling howl breaking the toe-chilling silence – and all the mythological baggage that goes with it.

I have been advised to be as quiet as possible so as not to frighten the wolves away – even to the point of not wearing nylon over-trousers because they make too much noise. What kind of advice is this? The nearest wolf is probably miles away, and since when were they so timorous? Surely there was a time when they had to be beaten off with sticks? If you were lucky. Literature is full of tales of people in horse-drawn sledges being pursued through the night by packs of ravening beasts, usually with unfortunate consequences. But I am told that all these stories are nonsense and that there has never been a single authenticated account of a non-rabid wolf attacking a human. If these people are to be believed, the wolf is a bit of a wuss.

ILLUSTRATION BY PETER BAILEY

It's the idea of wolves that's so potent – the heart-chilling howl breaking the toe-chilling silence – and all the mythological baggage that goes with it

It's still good to be here, with or without the wolves, as this is genuine Little Red Riding Hood and Hansel and Gretel territory: primeval pine and birch forest, and although the woodcutters now carry chainsaws and mobile phones, it has retained its ancient plant diversity with enough space between the trees for moss, wildflowers, snow drifts and wildlife. And the past is lurking only a few yards off the path: an overgrown monument commemorates in Gothic script the actual spot where on 28 September 1912 Kaiser Wilhelm II shot his two thousandth stag.

We are staying in an old hunting lodge, now the chief forester's house, with lots of wood panelling hung with antlers, musty but reassuringly authentic smells and few unnecessary concessions to the twenty-first century. When guests are staying the forester's sister-in-law comes from the nearby town to do the cooking: good old-fashioned comfort food, with large helpings of fried pork, pickles and dumplings. One evening we have a wild boar barbecue beside a frozen lake accompanied by excessive amounts of mulled vodka.

Actually, it's nowhere near as cold in the high seat as it ought to be, only a few degrees below freezing. I have a bottle of bison grass vodka for company, which helps pass the time. The flavour is somewhat unusual, alarmingly similar to the smell of bison droppings – not an immediate choice as a food flavouring.

My fellow travellers are good company whose conversation is not confined to wisents and woodpeckers, always a danger on trips like this. They have all seen wild boar, elk, bison, various types of deer – and wolf. But I have not. Possibly because I was asleep at the time.

Around midnight, the wind gets up, shaking the high seat. The snow is now coming down heavily. A pattern is emerging: sleep for ten minutes, wake up in acute discomfort, scan the meadow for five minutes, fail to see anything, fall asleep.

One thing I have learned while I've been here is that wolves prefer to walk along existing tracks rather than make their way through thick forest. So when Little Red Riding Hood's parents told her not to leave the path they were making it more, not less, likely that she would have an encounter with the wolf. What conclusion can be drawn from that?

At around 4 am I am rewarded by the sight of a whole herd of zilch moving silently across the snowy meadow. Zilch are native to much of Eastern Europe but are particularly revered in this part of the former East Prussia. In times of hardship they formed the staple diet of the population.

At 8 am, on the way back to the lodge, we find fresh wolf tracks in the snow, only a couple of minutes old. Round the corner is the spot where it stopped to listen to our approach before taking evasive action, and I become aware that some where nearby, possibly very close, a pair of eyes are watching every move I make.

'Go to sleep, dear, or the childcare professionals will come and get you'

Notes from the sofa

Socialising: why make a meal out of it?

Written and illustrated by **RAYMOND BRIGGS**

DINNER PARTIES. God spare us. Did we ever do them, once upon a time? Yes, we did. Why? Did we really enjoy them? Or was it just a habit, an obligation, almost a duty?

Nowadays, they are unthinkable. When Liz and I sit on the sofa, semi-comatose after our evening meal, and I am wondering if it's worth heaving myself off the cushions to flog all the way across the room to get the *Radio Times*, I sometimes say to Liz: 'Do you realise that this is dinner-party arriving time? Any moment now, six people would come smiling in, bearing wine, gifts and flowers.' 'Oh, don't,' she says weakly. We would all then chatter drunkenly till midnight and beyond. Also, in those days, the room would be choked with smoke. It still stank when we staggered down in the morning to face the mountain of washing-up.

Insanity. Does any oldie still practise this lunatic ritual? Do the young still do it? Those under sixty, I mean.

First would come The Planning ... who would go with whom ... better be careful ... wasn't she having a bit of a go with him? Did her husband know? No, but his wife did. Better leave it ...

Then, The Date ... endless phoning to find a time when eight people were all free on the same evening.

Then, The Recipes ... no, we can't do that, this lot have had it before ... no, not that, Angela's done it twice ... and she's brilliant at it ... (there was always a slight air of competition).

Then came The Shopping ... for weird ingredients we'd never heard of ...

Then, oh spare us, The Cooking ... anxiety ... nervous tension ... rows ... divorce?

When we were really young – students and twenties – an evening meal with friends was a treat. Gosh! A bottle of wine! And a foreign recipe! (Elizabeth David, Penguin, 2/6d!) Spaghetti not out of a tin. Oh, really? It's called pasta, is it?

Then later, in middle age, everyone was eating in restaurants all the time, usually to do with work, so it was no longer a treat to have fancy foreign food.

Many years ago, I wrote to all our friends saying that, due to increasing decrepitude, would they mind if we dropped the dinner-party habit, and suggested we meet for tea instead, as the main point of any gathering was the people, not the food.

It's so long ago now, I can't remember what became of the idea. We certainly stopped giving dinner parties. Can't remember the teas either... but then even tea parties are rather tiresome, aren't they?

Perhaps we're getting old.

Too long in the tooth

Scottish enthusiasts may be delighted to welcome back the beaver with its love of stripping bark and damming streams, but **CHARLES ELLIOTT** *takes a darker view*

Illustration by Martin Honeysett

Beavers are cute. Well, maybe not quite as cute as otters – especially the ones you see on television sliding on their backs down a muddy bank like gamin four-year-olds. But quirky and attractive, anyway. Watch one swimming towards you with a small branch clutched in its buck teeth, its pug nose just above the water, its little eyes beaming at you out of a helmet of sleek fur – why, you just have to smile! Add to that the beaver's utterly unimpeachable credentials – vegetarian, uxorious – and you have a thoroughly delightful creature. Who would not wish to encourage his presence among us?

I would. I have a history with beavers. So do a lot of my fellow Americans. The European beaver (*Castor fiber*) has been extinct in Britain for at least two hundred years, mainly the victim of hunters who prized its sleek pelt, its meat, and the musk gland secreting a substance used in medicine and perfume making. Last spring, however, three families were released into the Knapdale wilderness area near the Sound of Jura in Argyll under the benevolent auspices of the Scottish Beaver Trial partnership in the hope that they would reproduce and thrive. Plans are afoot to do the same in England and Wales in the next few years once suitable habitats have been identified; candidates under consideration include the New Forest, Bodmin Moor, and the Forest of Bowland in Lancashire.

So the prospect is for plenty of what Michael Russell, the transfixed Scottish Environment Minister, calls these 'charismatic, resourceful little mammals' to be snuffling all across the country before long. Is that a good idea? A number of landowners and fishermen in Scotland thought not, and managed to delay the scheme for a decade or so. They worried about destroyed forests and blocked salmon rivers, but in the end were unable to defeat the wildlife lobby.

In theory, the Knapdale experiment is intended as a carefully monitored trial run, although the remote, uninhabited nature of the area may not tell much about the dangers involved in loosing beavers in more settled regions. In any case, the protestors have not given up.

Nor should they, in my opinion. The world already has quite enough beavers, and in some places far too many. My own bias against them probably stems from the time I was scared witless while fishing one night in pitch darkness on the shore of Yellowstone Lake; a beaver smashed his flat tail on the surface a yard or two in front of me, and it sounded like someone throwing a log in the water – but I was a mile from camp, alone. I only learned later who the guilty party was.

'Oh dear, this plant doesn't look too healthy'

The beaver has utterly unimpeachable credentials – vegetarian, uxorious. Who would not wish to encourage its presence among us? I would. I have a history with beavers.

Nevertheless, I have better reasons than timidity for objecting to beavers. I've lived in New England, I've seen what *Castor canadensis*, our beavers' American brothers, can do to the landscape. Their predilection for damming streams can back up stagnant ponds ('beaver flows') capable of drowning square miles of forest. Attacks on riverside vegetation can leave broadleaf trees looking like the Argonne after the battle. (Beavers need bark and greenery to eat, and like other rodents, their four giant incisors keep on growing all their lives. The growth amounts to a millimetre a day, and if they didn't gnaw assiduously their teeth would get out of control.) In more settled urban areas they can flood sewage systems, undermine buildings and kill amenity trees. Moreover – despite the nonchalant claims of the introduction proponents – they multiply. In 1900 there were about 100,000 beavers left in North America, almost all of them in Canada. Today there are estimated to be ten to fifteen million.

In June 2009 the *New York Times* reported a meeting of desperate city officials in Concord, just west of Boston. Septic tanks were being wrecked, culverts clogged, residents reduced to painting trees with a mixture of paint and grit to discourage gnawing. What, they pleaded with conservation experts, could be done? Not much, was the answer. 'Beavers are the ultimate eco-system engineers.'

★ Great Bores of Today ★

'... Ellie's working two days a week in a wine bar and she's just come back from a fortnight in Corfu with my ex to recover from her AS levels and tomorrow she's flying to Botswana with a group of school friends where they're doing a cycle ride to raise money for Save the Whales and Nick is in Peru backpacking across the Andes with his new girl-friend and two other friends of hers Mollie and Mark from Cambridge and when he comes back he's going straight off to Norway to help plant sustainable forests then in September he's off to Manchester to do law their life is so exciting isn't it...? '

East of Islington

The unusual life of Sam Taylor and friends

It's all Greek to him...

Fungus Friend finds lust among the crashing crockery

Fungus Friend liked to think of himself as a man of the world. He ate pizza. He drank French wine, when he wasn't paying. He often wore a specially commissioned safari suit with monogrammed epaulettes, and always made a point of talking very loudly in perfect English when approached by confused foreigners in search of directions.

But his allegiance to the global village really came into its own while pursuing his favourite pastime: ensnaring unsuspecting females. 'They need guidance,' he was fond of saying when introduced to the naïve, newly arrived, eastern European au pairs employed by his more successful friends.

No nation was safe from a potential invasion. Spanish, German, Scandinavian, Slavic – he had, he liked to boast, 'been there, done that'. But not the inventors of democracy. For some reason the Greeks had always refused his attempts at romantic diplomacy. Until now, that is.

He had been invited to a friend's fiftieth birthday party, an occasion that the man's wife believed gave her an excuse to smash large quantities of crockery, all helpfully provided by the restaurateur and paid for by her husband. By the time dessert arrived, the floor was literally awash with the shattered remains of hundreds of once perfectly serviceable plates and the tears of the man footing the bill.

Which was when the restaurant door was flung open and in walked Zorbina, the proprietor's sister. Bold, raven-haired, she was, as far as Fungus Friend was concerned, the epitome of a Greek goddess.

Wasting little time, he crunched his way over to her table and introduced himself. 'Let me take you away from all this,' he said to her. Whereupon she threw a plate at his feet, which he took to be a yes. Zorbina, it transpired, was no wallflower, and several glasses of ouzo later, Fungus Friend discovered that she been married, had had several children, the exact number he was unsure about, and liked her men to be men. The latter she denoted by raising her bent arm in the air and pumping her muscle, Popeye style.

Real conversation was limited, not least because she had only arrived from Crete the day before and was just two pages into her Berlitz self-help language course. He needn't have worried though, she clearly had a way of making her feelings felt and had somehow managed to master a few select phrases.

Zorbina was bold and raven-haired and, as far as Fungus Friend was concerned, the epitome of a Greek goddess

The primary one seemed to be 'Huh, waster,' which she spat out every time the subject of her ex-husband arose. And 'filth', which she seemed to think meant the same thing as 'Cheers!' However, as she used it whenever she downed a glass of neat ouzo, Fungus Friend concluded that it was just possible that she had properly mastered that one.

After a couple of hours of sitting together and not talking, Fungus Friend felt confident that the relationship was proceeding quite well, and suggested that they go back to his flat for a nightcap. Although a state of near bankruptcy forced him to share a small flat with a large number of other people, he was sure they would be asleep, leaving the coast clear for him and Zorbina to continue reading each other's body language in peace.

Miraculously, she seemed amenable and so they set off, with Fungus Friend carrying her incredibly large bag, the contents of which seemed very vague. Within moments of them being in the door, much to his surprise, passion overtook her and she fell into his arms, and onto his badly made bed.

Like a scene from a Hollywood movie, they rolled around in a frenzy, the static from his nylon sheets barely competing with the red hot heat of their fervour. Then, just at the moment when Fungus Friend thought the waves were about to start crashing onto the shore, Zorbina leapt up and pulled a bouzouki out of her vast bag. In an ecstatic trance-like state, for which he felt he could get some credit, she began playing, loudly.

Within moments the entire household was awake and in his room. But Zorbina was oblivious, she was determined to finish. Eventually, after what seemed an eternity, but which was actually only ten minutes, there was silence. The flatmates, dazed and confused, clapped.

Zorbina smiled and shouted 'Filth!'

'If only!' Fungus Friend cried.

The Oldie 18 years of cover art

Artist and year, clockwise from top left: Bob Wilson, September 2008; Axel Scheffler, Summer 2009; Quentin Blake, March 1993; Ham Khan, March 2005; Posy Simmonds, August 2001; Steven Appleby, June 1992; Ralph Dobson, January 2010; Ed McLachlan, March 2006

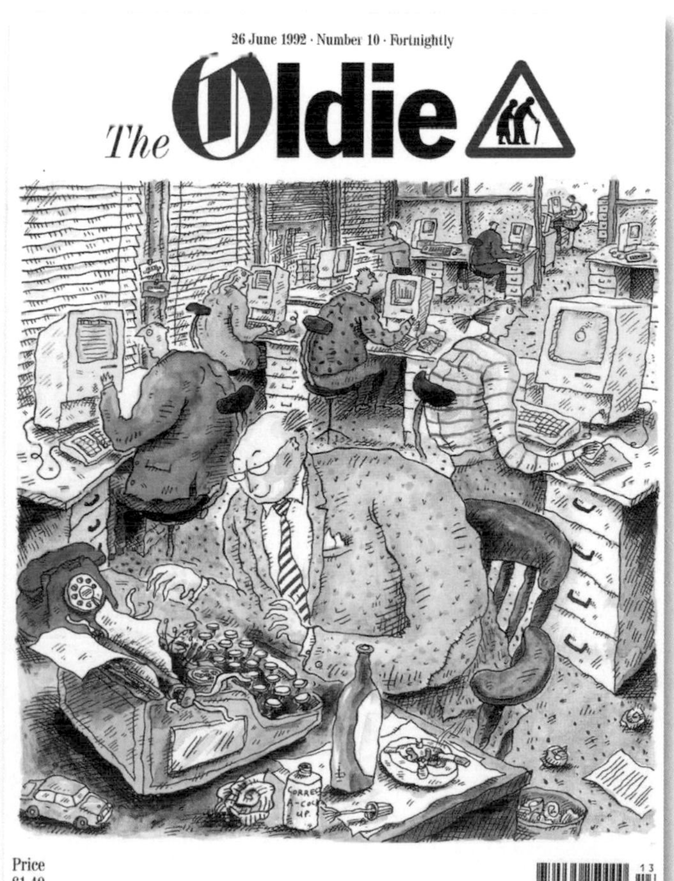

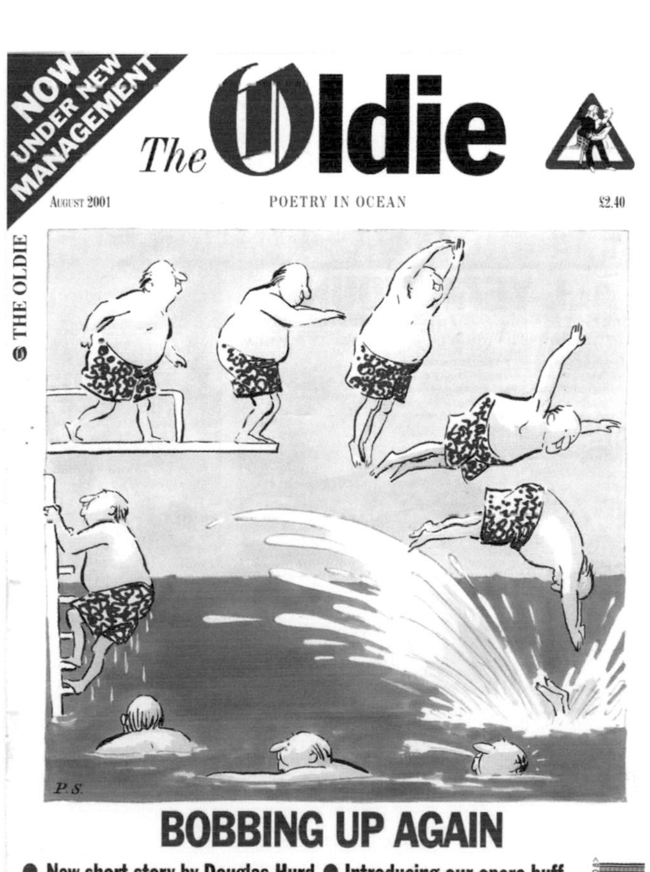

It's plumb crazy!

Pipes, pressure and plugholes: has **SARA WHEELER** *found a new vocation after going on a half-day plumbing course?*

Veteran readers might recall my previous attempts as an impecunious writer to acquire lucrative new skills. The bills still tumbled through the letter box, so I went on a plumbing course.

A friend had told me about Staunch and Flow, a West London-based plumbing firm which had inaugurated a series of half-day starter-courses. I booked myself in and went into the living room to tell my husband, who unfolded his arms and opened one eye (he was lying on the sofa listening to *Gardeners' Question Time*). He had shown no interest in my earlier belly-dancing or stripping prowess. 'Ah, a spot of plumbing,' he purred, trying to imitate Peter O'Toole in the strip club scene in *What's New, Pussycat?*

The course took place in the second-floor of Goslett's, an old family plumbing merchants situated close to the roar of the Westway. I was greeted on arrival by Staunch and Flow's Richard Nissen, an avuncular figure wielding a cafetière (for there was no builders' tea here). He turned out to be a plumber with a mission, the Bob Geldof of the U-bend. 'We can make a difference!' he enthused, balancing the cafetière on the lip of a bidet.

'We designed the course primarily to give you leverage when you call the plumber, so you aren't ripped off.' Every course takes a maximum of ten students, enabling each to benefit from one-to-one attention. My group included Simon, a fifty-odd gent in jeans and a chalk-striped jacket who complained of a hangover from too much champagne at the opera the night before. A young man wearing what looked like a denim profiterole on his head was a recent engineering graduate. Two more were mothers of small children keen on blocking the lav with toys.

Richard began by handing out a glossary of terms backed up with helpful cribsheets divided into two columns, headed 'What Your Plumber Says' and 'What You Say' (he says the F and E, you say the small tank in the loft, and you both mean the Feed and Expansion Cistern, which supplies the radiator circuit). It is crucial, it turns out, to know the difference between a sink and a basin. A sink, said Richard, only exists in a kitchen. 'Or a bootroom,' Simon chipped in. The diameter of the pipes is different, so if you use the wrong term, the plumber arrives with the wrong pipe.

The teacher of my plumbing course turned out to be a plumber with a mission: the Bob Geldof of the U-bend

And so it went on. Richard produced a variety of plumbing parts, passing them round for us to fondle. He was a natural teacher, expounding the secrets of sewerage with an enthusiasm rarely seen in the world of ballcocks. 'This is a waste pipe, or trap,' he said, holding up a wiggly plastic tube, 'a really huge invention by the Victorians!' This device goes under the sink, and a puddle of water in the bend prevents bad smells making their way back up the pipe. The old-fashioned variety is much better than the sexy-looking bottletrap that architects now want you to use. 'If grains of rice go down the plughole,' Richard explained, 'a bottletrap fills up.'

This, it seemed to me, would be useful information were one installing a new kitchen. Over the course of the morning other points emerged to indicate that the design-led obsessions of architects are frequently contrary to plumbing common sense – invisible controls without access panels, for example. But the fancy ideas

ILLUSTRATION BY ARTHUR ROBINS

'So you're his fancy woman!'

of architects are as nothing compared to the legislative meddling of government.

'We have always had lower water pressure than almost any other country,' Richard explained. 'The government has forced Thames Water to reduce London's pressure still further in order to reduce leakage and therefore be environmentally friendly. It means the pressure in some places now isn't even high enough to reach the top of a building. It's a case of government pressure screwing up the pressure.' And because Britain industrialised first, we put in lead pipes, which makes our eco-capability different from that of our Continental neighbours – a fact not recognised by regulations flowing from Brussels.

After a lecture on what to do in emergencies (how to turn off the water, for example, when your gate valve shears off), we were taught how to solve basic domestic plumbing problems. Finally, Richard issued a catalogue of prophylactic advice. Nail guns for trendy blond wood floors apparently account for a high percentage of plumbing callouts, as they pierce pipes.

'Check your flooring contractor is paying attention,' we were counselled. 'And don't buy plumbing gear from B & Q.'

I returned home determined to tackle a bath tap that had been leaking since we moved in four years ago. To my amazement, I successfully changed the washer. I was thrilled. This was way better than stripping! My husband was so impressed that he got off the sofa. Later that day I found him in front of the computer searching the internet to find out how he could get me CORGI-registered.

Not so grim Up North

Life in the Pennines

Illustrated by Peter Brook

THERE ARE occasions in every year when our parish church is full, without a single empty seat, but they do not include Easter or Christmas, well attended though those festivals are. Apart from certain funerals, the one sure event that everyone tries to attend is Remembrance Sunday, which may have varied in national popularity over the past few decades but has never been regarded here as anything less than a solemn day of obligation in our calendar. It would be a brave (and deeply insensitive) body who didn't come to church then without a poppy on their coat.

Its ritual is unvarying, and has been ever since the first Armistice Day service was held, the year after the Great War ended. Nowadays, as the church is filling up, the old sweats from the Second World War fall in outside the Market Hall and march down the street to join the rest of us, not quite like the metronomes they once were in uniform, but doing their best to keep their arms straight and their legs striding as one.

For twenty years or so their numbers have dwindled steadily, but there's still a handful left, including Jim, who was at El Alamein and survived to run our garage. There also used to be Frank, who achieved international recognition (we still sometimes see him in news clips on television) as the young soldier with a handkerchief over his nose and mouth, sitting on top of his bulldozer and shoving naked corpses into open graves after Belsen concentration camp was liberated in 1945. The lad spent his 21st birthday doing that, wondering how on earth he had come to be in such a hell-hole when his normal habitat was a version of Paradise.

The old sweats wear their medals, of course, and we once had a vicar who was so determined not to be upstaged that he pinned to his surplice the little gong he'd been given as honorary chaplain to the Leeds Sea Cadets. The rest of us just dress darkly and flaunt that splash of crimson on our lapels. Our Prize Silver Band is assembled in the Lady Chapel, to augment the organ at the singing of hymns – 'Onward Christian Soldiers', 'Oh, Valiant Hearts', 'Eternal Father', and the recessional 'Guide Me Oh Thou Great Redeemer': we have no wish to depart from the traditional. The British Legion banner and the White Ensign of a warship once named after this dale are laid on the altar till the end of the service. We are handing on a torch.

The most solemn moment comes when our priest recites the names of the forty-nine men from this parish who never came home again, chiefly from the Great War, when the total population of the town, its surrounding villages and the hamlets of the Upper Dale would have been something less than two thousand souls. Then Brian takes his cornet from the Lady Chapel to the west end of the church and sounds the Last Post and the Reveille with a tonic brilliance that has never been bettered at the Cenotaph or anywhere else. And another spellbound moment passes into our history.

It has been so for the past ninety years, and it will be so again this November. As we were reminded in the sermon preached at last year's Remembrance Sunday, the names will be read once more 'while we turn them over in our memories and promise ourselves – and them – that they will never be forgotten in this place'.

GEOFFREY MOORHOUSE

Unwrecked England

Uppingham, Rutland

Candida Lycett Green

Uppingham is a cracking little town. Its heart is all Oxford marmalade-coloured stone, its shops gloriously independent and its famous school exudes an air of academia and comfortable stability – a microcosm of a university city. The town stands high on a plateau (as the 'Up' in its name suggests) amidst ravishing farmland: proper rolling country of small fields set with hedgerow trees, copses, little woods and hill-top villages like Gretton and Seaton. It's as though twentieth-century farming practices have passed it by, for there are no huge expanses where eight fields have been made into one. It would be hard to find a more truly English slice of country than this bit of Rutland.

Through dark gold Rockingham, and over the lost Oakham to Kettering railway line, whose 82 arched viaducts still march across the low-lying river meadows of the Welland, the main road sweeps dead north. Suddenly, with no warning, after a short hill climb, you are right in the old centre of Uppingham, its medieval street-pattern virtually unchanged. The High Street, once the main thoroughfare from Leicester to Peterborough, strikes across from east to west and the town's later, settled suburbs spread away on either side of the road leading out towards Oakham.

Above: High Street, Uppingham, in the snow

The scale of Uppingham is just right. Along the High Street there are old inns and clusters of handsome shops, some bow-fronted, some spreading their wares onto the pavement. Nelson's, one of the two butchers in town, is painted forest green with gold lettering and has been in the family since 1924. There are two classy second-hand bookshops in picturesque premises, and as a stranger I felt utterly at home wandering around or sitting outside Don Paddy's on the small market square. An ironmongers on the corner sports a gaily-painted hand plough above its grand, classical doorway

and coloured stained glass along the tops of the windows. The seventeenth-century Falcon Hotel with its Victorian façade encloses the north side of the square, and the parish church of St Peter and St Paul, the south. Jeremy Taylor, the seventeenth-century writer and rector of Uppingham, who was known as the 'Shakespeare of the Divines', gave lyrical sermons from the pulpit here, and close by is the original Uppingham School, founded in 1584.

When the Reverend Thring took over as headmaster in the 1850s he made sweeping changes, and after thirty-four years left a large and flourishing school housed in some of the finest school buildings in the country. Quadrangles of classroom blocks, library, chapel and hall dominate the west side of town. Thring employed the architect G E Street, and subsequent heads continued to uphold the high calibre of design by using celebrated architects of the day, such as Ernest Newton and Oliver Hill. The thatched Arts and Crafts cricket pavilion stands in what are today the largest school playing fields in England.

Its heart is all marmalade-coloured stone, its shops gloriously independent, and its famous school exudes an air of academia and comfortable stability

What I like best about Uppingham is that you are always so close to rurality. From being right in the middle of the bustling market square on a Friday, when the place is filled with stalls and The Vaults pub is humming, you can walk a few yards to the other side of the church and find yourself in the country. The sudden contrast is magical. A path slopes down through a little green beside a row of tiny ironstone cottages, Pinfold the tiniest of all, and just across the lane a secret path, tunnelled over with elder, may and ivy, leads past a pleasing patchwork of allotments over a trickle of a stream and up into undulating Rutland landscape.

PHOTOGRAPHS COURTESY OF THEODORA WAYTE

LEFT: Mira Bar-Hillel as an 18-year-old Israeli army conscript, 1964
ABOVE: An Israeli officer on his mobile phone, Israeli-Gaza border, 2008

Phone home, kid

What do you get when you combine an army of young conscripts with mobile phones and Jewish mothers? According to **MIRA BAR-HILLEL**, *a skewed military policy ...*

Imagine the scene, if you will. The battle rages at El Alamein or Waterloo. Suddenly the phone rings for Monty – or Wellington. The caller is a hysterical mother whose soldier son has just spoken to her on his mobile phone, describing the horrors all around him. 'I hold you personally responsible for his wellbeing,' she says to the general. 'Oh dear,' he thinks. 'Perhaps I should reconsider my battle plans...'

Absurd? Perhaps. But as a veteran of the Israeli army on holiday in Tel Aviv when the bombardment of Gaza began in 2008, I was forced to conclude that the mobile phone revolution is the only reasonable explanation for the fact that, while over 1,300 Gazans perished in the attack on Hamas, the number of Israeli army dead was ... ten.

When I was conscripted into the Israeli army in 1964, the country was – as usual – between wars. But it was subject to regular cross-border incursions by the kind of chaps who today would be simply labelled 'terrorists'. In those days they had other titles, mainly 'infiltrators', but their purpose was to damage and alarm the local (Israeli) population by use of force. And the army's clear purpose was to protect this civilian population at any cost, even to the death.

As conscripts, our lives were basic and harsh. Enlisted men slept in tents, women and NCOs in wooden huts, six to a room, and you had to be really hungry to eat the mess food. There was a lot of moaning, of course – but not to mum: in the absence of mobile phones, getting help from home was not an option, and it never occurred to us to try. Mum was someone you went home to when you got some leave, and when there you put a brave face on it and that was that.

While over 1,300 Gazans perished in the attack on Hamas, the number of Israeli army dead was ... ten

How things have changed. I found this out after I arrived in Israel just hours before the beginning of the attack on Gaza. The 'war' occupied the media full time, but the first time I heard ordinary people, in the relative safety of Tel Aviv, talking as though what was going on mattered deeply and personally to *them*, was ten days into the battle – when the first Israeli soldier died on entering Gaza on foot, after the air force failed to pound Hamas into submission from the air. I have since realised that, while in the rest of the world the role of the military is seen as the defender of civilian populations, in Israel things have somehow turned on their head.

It began during the 2006 ('second') Lebanon war when the entire northern part of Israel, including the third largest city, Haifa, was at the mercy of Hizbollah rockets for weeks on end. There were many casualties and daily life came to a standstill. Yet both the military authorities and the politicians were reluctant to follow the massive air strikes

– which had failed to halt Hizbollah's rocket attacks – with a ground invasion. The reason was the fear of what is now known as 'body-bag syndrome' – civilians were, in effect, sacrificed to prevent the deaths of soldiers.

I now know why this is so, and it has been explained and defended to me several times in the past few weeks by friends and relations whose children are – or have served – in the Israeli army and whose grandchildren will too. 'It's not "the army",' they tell me. 'It's *our kids*.' This is, of course, true. Young men (and, to a lesser extent, women) are still conscripted at the age of eighteen, and serve for around three years. Service is compulsory and unpaid – and so is fighting. It was ever thus, yet I cannot remember this 'soldiers first' phenomenon in any of the earlier wars which have dotted Israel's history since the first one, in 1948.

Back then, of course, the entirety of the Jewish nation became embroiled as its fledgling state was attacked by half a dozen Arab armies, their leaders incensed that the UN had voted to give the Jews, who had just lost six million of their numbers in the Holocaust, a safe haven of their own. But ever since then – in the Sinai campaign of 1956, the Six Day War of 1967 and the Yom Kippur War of 1973, not to mention the countless 'retaliatory' attacks on terrorist infiltrators over the decades – it was clearly the rôle of the army to defend the general population, not the other way round.

So what happened? Mobile phones happened. Israeli kids were among the first in the world to be given mobile phones by anxious parents. They got used to calling mum and dad whenever there was anything they wanted, needed – or feared. Conscripted at eighteen, they still call mum and dad. And mum and dad call their friends, who may be high-ranking military officers, MKs (Members of the Knesset) or cabinet ministers. It's a small country, and everybody seems to know everybody.

So how would Waterloo or El Alamein have been conducted had Wellington or Monty been at the receiving end of calls from their soldiers' mums? Is military strategy in the Middle East now being increasingly dictated by anxious Jewish mothers trying to protect their young at any cost? My gut feeling is that the answer is Yes. What the effect will be, time alone will tell.

Profitable Wonders

by James Le Fanu

The Earthworm

THE SEVENTEENTH-CENTURY metaphysical poet, Thomas Traherne, in the introduction to his major work, *Centuries of Meditations*, 'had a mind to fill it with Profitable Wonders'. Not, obviously, the profit of income over expenditure but rather the profit that is advantageous to those who recognise what it means to live in an enchanted world. 'You never enjoy the world aright till the sea itself flows in your veins, till you are clothed with the heavens and crowned with the stars,' he wrote, 'till you so love the beauty of enjoying it, you are earnest to persuade others to enjoy it too.'

For Traherne, there was nothing so commonplace that it would not command his attention. Here the obvious of our everyday lives becomes, on reflection, distinctly non-obvious. 'What diamonds are equal to my eyes, what gates of ivory to the double portal of my lips and teeth? Is not sight a jewel? Is not hearing a treasure? Is not speech a glory?'

And there is nothing so full of profitable wonder as the natural miracle of self-renewing life, marching down through the ages in such an abundance of shape, form, attributes and propensity as to encompass the full range, and more, of what might be possible. Why should the ten thousand species of birds yet be so readily distinguishable one from the other by their pattern of flight, or the shape of their wings, the colour of their plumage or the notes of their song?

'By their melodious accents they gratify our ears,' observed John Ray, the original 'twitcher', founder of the scientific discipline of ornithology and a direct contemporary of Traherne. 'By their beautiful shapes and colours they delight our eyes, without them the hedges and woods would be lonely and melancholy.'

Four hundred years on we should, by rights, be vastly more appreciative of such profitable wonders, for we now know so much more about the natural world and the deep complexities that underpin it. Yet one could search a shelf's worth of biology textbooks in vain for the slightest hint of the extraordinary in their detailed exposition of the facts of zoology and botany, anatomy, physiology or embryology. Science no longer does 'wonder', for it is in thrall to the belief that there is nothing in principle it cannot account for, where the unknown is merely waiting-to-be-known.

This presupposition of understanding, that would reduce the near-infinite diversity of life to the nuts and bolts, proteins and enzymes of which all living things are made, disenchants the world by propagating the illusion that we know so much more than we do, or can.

> ***The survival and prosperity of our species is utterly dependent on the labours of the humble earthworm***

It was not always thus, for biologists of preceding generations were inspired by the grander vision that 'the truth' lay rather in the intricate interdependency of the living world. Thus, the survival and prosperity of our species is, as J Arthur Thomson, the one-time Professor of Natural History at Aberdeen University, points out, utterly dependent on the labours of the humble earthworm – without whose exertions in aerating the dense, inhospitable soil there would never have been a single field of corn.

'When we pause to think of the part earthworms have played in the history of the earth, they are clearly the most useful of animals. By their burrowing they loosen the earth, making way for the plant rootlets and the raindrops; by bruising the soil in their gizzards they reduce the minimum particles to more useful forms. They were ploughers before the plough, five hundred thousand to an acre passing ten tons of soil every year through their bodies.'

Seasonal suicide notes

by **ROGER LEWIS**

Illustrated by **MARTIN HONEYSETT**

An erstwhile Fellow of Wolfson College, Oxford, Roger Lewis abandoned academia for the life of a freelance writer. He has written biographies of Peter Sellers, Charles Hawtrey (of *Carry On* fame) and, most controversially, Anthony Burgess. His *Seasonal Suicide Notes* started out as an antidote to the saccharine and self-important round robins sent out at Christmas.

West Country charm

Ned Sherrin obit. Ned looked exactly like what he was, a big lumpy pumpkin-faced farmer, a camp haymaker. Was it old Ned who, when in the West Country once, asked a cab driver to take him to a club, and the driver said very slowly, 'Thar baint be no bum in Wincanton'?

February 2008

Who he?

Anna and Tristan back after three weeks – just as well as I was getting so plastered and lonely I accessed Friends Reunited. Nobody responded, possibly because in the section where you had to write about yourself I typed, 'Look me up in *Who's Who*, sad loser bastards.' The children I grew up with are now variously van drivers and supermarket checkout supervisors. A pair of high-fliers became a dentist in Caerphilly and a police superintendent in Swansea. Talking of *Who's Who*, they have an impressive satire or bullshit monitor on the team, as my attempt to add my appearance on *The Bernie Clifton Show* to my list of achievements was disallowed.

August 2005

Evolution

Sébastien comes in through the door most days with his mobile in his hand, furiously texting. He and his cronies sit on the school bus, texting each other. Nobody takes the trouble to talk to each other properly anymore. Like, I am sure, every other adolescent of his generation, he completely ignores his parents. We could be the other side of a screen, not quite in focus. To get him to come down from his lair for dinner, I have to phone him up. I go for months without speaking to any of my editors too – all communication is done in cyberspace, briskly and brutally. I feel we shall soon evolve into blobby lumps (and I'm well on the way) with no extremities save prongs on our foreheads to tap the keyboard. Wit and fluency and conversation are going the way of thatching and sailing ships – quaint and outmoded skills. The best I now hope for from even intelligent fellows is an ill-spelled and ill-phrased three-line email. What do I mean *three lines*! I lately spent a few weeks polishing a long article. I proudly sent it off. Silence. Here in its entirety is the grudging response I got eventually: 'Ta.'

July 2008

Existentialism

Gyles Brandreth called in for lunch on his way to address the Oswestry branch of Bingo for the Deaf. I asked him if it is true that Sandi Toksvig is an Eskimo? He looked at me askance. I made him a cup of tea. 'This is the most wonderful cup of tea I have ever had in my life,' he said, so firmly I believed it. I opened the door to the dining-room and we proceeded to tuck in. 'This is the most wonderful lunch I have ever had in my life,' he claimed. Later on, Anna took him to Leominster Railway Station. 'This is the most wonderful lift I have ever had in my life,' I expected him to say in a heartfelt manner – and when the Arriva Trains Wales train pulled in, 'This is the most wonderful train I have ever seen in my life.' I suppose up until that very precise moment, such sentiments may well be true – and if from minute to minute and day to day you manage to exist positively and continuously in the present tense, they'll always be true. For myself, I can never stop being overwhelmed by the past and see only fiasco and anticlimax in prospect.

July 2007

Paedophile coming

A man at the leisure pool in Ross-on-Wye jostled his way past a group of primary school children saying as he went, 'Excuse me, paedophile coming through!' I thought this hugely funny – but of course the headteachers and local officials are up in arms, an emergency meeting of the Herefordshire Council's Cabinet was convened, and the swimming pool closed down.

August 2008

Way to go

One of my true regrets is that I never met Jennifer Paterson – though I suppose I did technically encounter her once, when I had luncheon at the *Spectator* during my younger years, where she was the cook. One of the other guests was Wendy Cope – or was it Posy Simmonds? Or Fleur Adock? I seem to recall a mannish, cross person coming in and out anyway – presumably that was Jennifer. Though a devout Pre-Vatican II Catholic, because of her chain-smoker's cough she always approached Mass in a holy terror of going into a spasm and choking to death, trying to swallow the wafer. Her nasty coughing if any foreign body touched her throat must have ruled out lots of things besides, though I've heard rumours that when making *Two Fat Ladies* she was liable to bang the cameramen's dinner gongs with abandon.

Those *Two Fat Ladies* shows are favourites of mine, though not entirely for the food. I enjoy the way Jennifer and Clarissa Dickson Wright waddle around Cornwall or Cirencester, always hovering on the brink of squabbling. They obviously couldn't stand each other, upstage each other shamelessly and tread maliciously on punch lines. The highlight is always when Jennifer has had one nip too many of the rum punch and starts singing, her bass deeper than soulster Isaac Hayes, who voiced Chef on *South Park*.

October 2008

Cancer of the soul

'Circus people are different from other people,' said Fellini. 'They have a bond, and people who love the circus have a bond.' When I announce that my eldest son is an apprentice clown with Zippo's, where he is dressing up daily in striped stockings and perfecting pratfalls, I get one of two reactions. Most people remember going to circuses as children and mention the sawdust, pageantry and pomp with huge delight. Others put on a fixed smile and say what kind of life is it really, with these long-haired greasy gypsy louts and scallywags sitting in damp caravans under pylons. I find this insufferably snobbish – I go off them right away. Just as I always bridle if people use the word circus pejoratively, to mean *chaos* or *shallowness*. These are the insecure people, who need pathetic little traditional signs and symbols of alleged success to justify their non-existences, who cling to the company motor cars and pension pots, who are in thrall to sales figures and targets, the nine-till-five time-and-motion arsewipes who have Stage IV cancer of the soul.

August 2008

● ***Seasonal Suicide Notes: My Life As It Is Lived*** **by Roger Lewis, Short Books, £7.99, PB**

Face-off: Johnny Rotten (left) and Bill Grundy on the *Today* show, 1st December 1976

Grouch *on the* couch

Presenter Bill Grundy could frighten a guest off his sofa with fifteen seconds to go before live broadcast. **PETER WHEELER** *remembers him with affection and horror*

Bill Grundy's television career began in the late Fifties when he got a job as a newsreader on the newly fledged Granada Television channel. By the Sixties and Seventies he had become a well-known Granada presenter, but he is probably best remembered for his two-minute Sex Pistols interview, which was broadcast live on Thames Television's *Today* show during peak family viewing time on 1st December 1976.

Within seconds of the introduction, Grundy's mocking tone had elicited responses from band members Johnny Rotten and Steve Jones which included the words 'fuck' and 'shit'. Things rapidly degenerated when his inappropriate remark to the young Siouxsie Sioux – 'Let's meet afterwards, shall we?' – led to a shower of verbal abuse from Steve Jones of the 'dirty bastard' type, culminating in the clincher, 'What a fucking rotter'.

The tabloids had a field day, Grundy was suspended, and *Today* was axed shortly thereafter.

Although this incident virtually ended his TV career, it was, in the eyes of many, not his fault at all. Anyone conducting a studio interview is entitled to rely on support from the control gallery if matters get seriously out of hand. It is completely within the reach of the director and the crew to take the studio off the air at any moment, whereas the interviewer has only limited options for remedial action. Grundy was left to fend for himself in finding a way to end the Sex Pistols' foul-mouthed outpourings. In saying to Jones, 'Keep going, chief, keep going. Go on, you've got another five seconds. Say something outrageous,' Grundy was being sarcastic; far from encouraging them, he was being scornful and disapproving of their performance. His reaction to their vulgarity was wrongly assessed and misjudged by those whom it suited to blame him.

At the height of his career, Bill was one of Granada's star presenters and an accomplished exponent of Granada's mission to be different to the BBC. To take just one incident, shortly after the station launched, a royal event was covered. Whereas a BBC Dimbleby would have reported in hushed tones that 'The Queen can be seen receiving a bouquet', Bill's approach for Granada was to remark that 'Someone has just handed the Queen a bunch of flowers'.

He and Bill Crozier, fresh back from the British Forces Broadcasting Service in Germany, set about presenting the GTV early-evening magazine programme, *People and Places*, in a style that ran entirely counter to the BBC treatment of regional current affairs. They were fortunate to have, among others, Judith Chalmers to keep them under control, because an unrestrained Grundy could make a loose cannon look like a water pistol.

People and Places gave way to the more sophisticated *Scene at Six Thirty*, and I will never forget the evening on which Bill was to interview the Tory Minister Iain Macleod as the main live guest. As the studio settled down, a minute or so before transmission the floor manager asked Bill to put a question and get a reply so that the sound engineer could get a balance on their voices. Bill prevaricated until there was less than fifteen seconds to go before putting the extraordinary question, 'Mr Macleod, is there any truth in the rumour that you suffer from dandruff of the crotch?' A stunned silence and an odd calm overtook the studio as Iain Macleod rose from his chair without replying and walked out. Bill simply remarked to the floor manager that 'Our guest seems to have gone'. And with that, we were on the air with a large hole in the programme. I can't now remember how we filled the planned duration of that interview, but – in the best Elvis Presley tradition – Mr Macleod had 'left the building'.

I enjoyed working with Bill for many years on a BBC Radio programme called *Sport Spotlight*. It was on a very wet Saturday that he returned from the match on which he was reporting, more drenched than anyone I have ever seen. When I cued his report, he was sitting, still soaking wet, across the microphone with a malevolent expression on his face. His opening words said it all: 'Sound the Lutine Bell – I have to report a naval disaster.' It was the most graphic description of a washed-out football game that I heard in twelve years of fronting that programme.

Sport Spotlight was a tight ship under the command of Tony Preston, who, in a previous phase of his life, had been the adjutant of the Gloucesters in Korea. Tony was one of the last of a dying breed of officer and gentleman. Imagine his anguish after he invited Bill to compile a lively report on a Boxing Day meet of the Cheshire Hunt. Bill's piece was typically robust and spiced with several luck-pushing comments. The one that caused the strongest reaction was when he said, 'You always know that it is the Cheshire Hunt you are watching because the horses are better-looking than the women.' That comment was, of course, damaging enough, but made infinitely worse by the fact that the meet on which he was reporting had, in fact, been cancelled because of bad weather. When called to account by Tony, Bill was as unrepentant as ever, saying 'Well that explains why I couldn't find it.'

Bill walked the plank more frequently than most, but somehow he always had the ability to clamber back. It was when reading the news at Granada that he made television history by being the only newscaster ever to disappear from view by taking an alcohol-induced slide off his chair. The cameraman had the unenviable choice of keeping his shot on an empty seat or following his performer to the floor. In the event, the camera dipped momentarily but then returned to the vacant chair. Thankfully, the sound was faded out.

When reading the news at Granada he made television history by being the only newscaster ever to disappear from view by taking an alcohol-induced slide off his chair

The long-running GTV programme *All Our Yesterdays* (on which I was the voice of Churchill for eleven years) brought Bill and an old sparring partner, Brian Inglis, together. The unlikely mix of the mercurial Bill as producer and the urbane Brian as performer, worked very well. Bill's skills as a broadcast journalist and Brian's completely unruffled approach combined superbly. When the run was coming to an end, we realised that we had built up an unrivalled sound archive of World War Two, so Bill researched and I produced an LP, which eventually matured into a CD of the 'Sounds of All Our Yesterdays'.

All careers have embarrassing moments. And although Bill's had more to choose from than most, I suspect that the top slot is not hard to fill. It was not suffered on the air but in a favourite Granada watering hole where he made an ill-judged remark about the sexual orientation of a fellow producer. The reaction was swift and unexpected: a left hook that came from nowhere put Bill briefly on the floor. That might have been the end of the matter, but the denouement came the following morning when his assailant sent him a single rose by way of reconciliation.

Bill could anchor the coverage of a political conference for seven hours as well as, if not better than, anyone else in the business, without once faltering or losing a salient fact. He could hold a programme together when the 'technicals' were falling around him like leaves in autumn. It is fair to say that he never put out a dull programme in his life – and that's quite a tribute.

I remember him with a mixture of great affection, admiration and horror. He feared no one, and unfailingly represented the interests of his audience. Inevitably, on many occasions, this led to an abrasive style. But as I look at some of the sycophants on the sofa in today's magazine programmes, I realise just how much is still owed to the pioneering style set by Bill Grundy – the original grouch on the couch.

Iraq Triptych

Doing it the HARD WAY

Michael Sandle RA, our finest commemorative sculptor, denounces War, Blair, Conceptualism and Tate Modern. Interview by **JOHN McEWEN**

Michael Sandle

Sculpture can mean anything these days, so who stands for the sculptural tradition that has served the world so well for so long? In England it is 74-year-old Michael Sandle RA, the most challenging and finest commemorative sculptor of his generation. Sandle's memorials should be widespread, but they remain treasured exceptions. Part of the reason is that he has worked abroad for most of his career, as a leading professor of sculpture in Germany; but the main explanation is that he does and says what he thinks.

Anyone who doubts his credentials should look at his fierce *Saint George and the Dragon* at 2 Dorset Rise, Blackfriars; or his ghostly *Seafarers Memorial* (as memorable inside as out) jutting from the façade of the International Maritime Organisation headquarters on Albert Embankment; and, beyond London, his *Mighty Blow for Freedom* (also called *Fuck the Media*) at Milton Keynes; or, most magnificent of all, his semi-architectural *Malta Siege-Bell Memorial*, which tolls the noontime in Valetta every day.

There is also his monumental indoor diatribe against war, *A Twentieth-Century Memorial*, showing a skeletal Mickey Mouse manning a larger-than-life-size replica of a Browning machine-gun. It is in the Tate collection and was shown in the Duveen galleries before going to Halifax's Dean Clough. It should always be on display as a masterpiece of post-war art, but the Tate's Maoist permanent-revolution hanging policy usually condemns it to the stores.

What most distinguishes Sandle as an artist? Colin Amery best summed it up when he opened the superb retrospective at Ludlow Castle in 2007: 'Sandle's work is tough because – unlike the temporarily fashionable contemporary artists – it is about morality.' Sandle accepts this interpretation: 'I have a tendency to moral outrage. I've had it all my life.'

Art for him is a heroic calling and he minces no words in defending it. In 1997 he resigned from the Royal Academy over its inclusion of a portrait of Myra Hindley against the wishes of one of the mothers whose child Hindley had murdered. Eventually the Academy cajoled him to return.

His art is much concerned with war, an astonishingly neglected subject in this most barbaric of all the ages. Sandle does not deny that his obsession has a self-expressive side: 'I've often used the notion of war as a metaphor for my own struggle and conflict.' But he is always motivated by events: the two world wars, Vietnam, the Falklands conflict and Iraq.

The villain of Iraq is Blair, whom Sandle would like to see tried for war crimes. 'I knew the moment he was elected leader of the Labour Party that this was a most dangerous man – no sense of history, no culture, a complete philistine, but most of all because he was mixing up politics and faith – after all, the SS had "*Gott mit uns*" on their belts. And now he's peddling religious platitudes through his Faith Foundation. He uses religion as an air-freshener to cover the stench of the rotting flesh he has caused. As for being a Middle East peace envoy, it's like employing King Herod to be a child minder.'

Sandle's disgust is vented in two memorable pieces: *Iraq Triptych* and *Iraq: The Sound of Your Silence*. The huge triptych (which won the Hugh Casson Prize for Drawing at the Royal Academy Summer Exhibition in 2007) shows the Blairs as a naked Adam and Eve cast out from No 10 into a world raining fragments of bodies onto mounds of corpses. The image went round the world but not a squeak was heard from the objects of his derision.

At 2009's Summer Exhibition he brought an even heavier gun to bear on 'the obscenity of the war' in the form of a lime-wood 'madonna', *Iraq: The Sound of Your Silence*, a three-times-lifesize carving of a seated woman awaiting execution. She has a blindfold in the form of a hood and, but for the indignity of her exposed breasts, is draped in a robe. On her lap she bears the swaddled corpse of her murdered baby, the pitiful stump of one raised arm showing the child is a war victim.

Iraq: The Sound of Your Silence

That this accusatory and compassionate sculpture was not placed in the middle of the rotunda as the centrepiece of the show only confirmed the silence it condemns. Instead it was sidelined in the adjacent Lecture Room, the place of honour given to the non-member Damien Hirst – surprise, surprise – with a made-to-order piece of figurative bling cast in silver.

The villain of Iraq is Blair, whom Sandle would like to see tried for war crimes

Sandle's carving, which weighs 400 kilos and took him three years to do, is deliberately hands on: 'There are a lot of contemporary artists whose work is abysmal because they haven't touched it themselves. They make a sketch or a rough maquette and get technicians to do it for them. I'm totally against that. The living presence of the artist is the art. *Iraq* is intended to be a smash in the face of conceptualism.'

The combination of a Blairite disdain for history and the get-rich-quick ethos in contemporary art offends him on every count. 'It reflects a consumer society which is incredibly corrupt and mentally wasteful. I lose the will to live when I see most of the stuff done today. It's so vacuous, so sterile, so derivative. I want art to reach me and tell me something. To find *that* I have to go to the National Gallery. I'm saturated in art history. For me this carving represents a continuum. I'm not into commerce and corporate art. I don't do it for money. I don't want to be a "conceptual artist". I want to be a real artist.'

His breadth of reference is the wider for his having lived so long abroad. The continuum includes the Gothic masters of German woodcarving and the Spanish baroque carvers. He was pleased to be described recently as 'a baroque artist'. With specific reference to *Iraq*, he also cites the influence of Matisse, Epstein and Diego Rivera. As an academician he regards it as an obligation to respect and safeguard the hard-earned lessons of tradition, while being true to himself, as all genuine artists are. 'The older I get the easier it is to go against the tide because the tide is going to turn anyway.'

He regards Tate Modern as an icon of 'Stalinist' culture – '"Stalinist" because the rules in the present "art game" are arbitrary and absolute.' For a long time he has fantasised about hijacking HMS *Belfast* and shelling Tate Modern to the ground.

On past form, that might just happen.

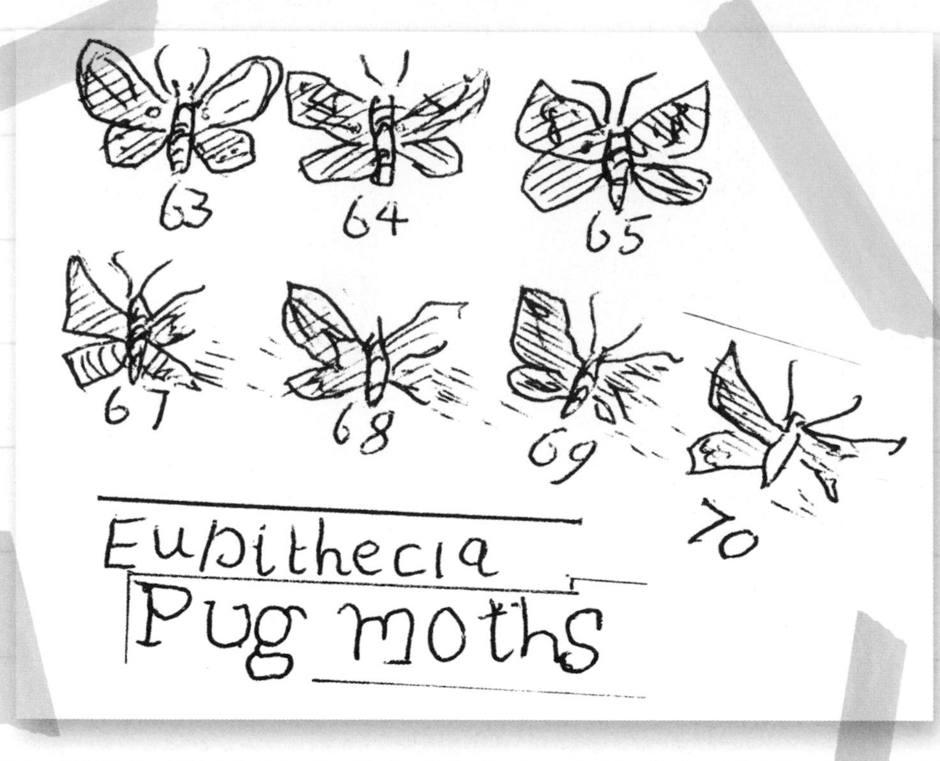

House Husbandry

with Giles Wood

In which Mr Wood stands up for nocturnal Lepidoptera

When a neighbour asked what had been the bright light blazing from my field throughout the previous night, I told him it was my newly bought moth trap. 'Good job too,' he retorted.

Wrong reaction. Little did he know I am trapping moths – briefly – for the purposes of identification, and then letting them go unharmed. I thought it hardly worth explaining this to him. One, he is deaf, and two, like too many Britons, he has a prejudice against moths.

Why do they get such a bad press? After all it is not the moth that wreaks havoc among clothes, carpets and fruit trees but its larvae. This technicality was clearly lost on Miles Coverdale when, translating the Bible into English, he wrote 'Lay not up treasures for yourselves upon this earth, where moth and rust doth corrupt...'

But there is also a general atavistic fear of all flapping nocturnal creatures which break into the lit rooms of suburban man at night.

What struck me forcibly on my first night's moth trapping was that here I was in my own private woodland but it did not belong to me, or the mortgage company, it belonged to the moths. Illuminated by the strong light from below the trees, each moth had a different flight pattern, some zooming, some fluttering, as if they were responding to different rates of gravity. As they negotiated the lattice-work of twigs and leaves they recalled tiny fish progressing through the intricacy of a coral reef.

With nine hundred resident species of macro moths, getting to know them is a testing task

The moth trap (under £300 from Watkins & Doncaster) acts like a very efficient lobster pot. Few moths can resist the powerful attraction of the mercury bulb and most dive straight into the trap, from where they can be released in the morning after identification, having spent a comfortable night in the recesses of inverted egg cartons.

Why bother? Some readers will remember the phenomenon of the 'moth snowstorms', when drivers used to have to stop to wipe the thick coating of dead moths off the headlights. Now, two thirds of the common larger moth species are in decline. My neighbour would say that's progress, but he has not heard ant expert EO Wilson express his view that 'if insects were to vanish from the earth the terrestrial environment would soon collapse into chaos'. And moths, just like bees, are a pollinating species although, for some reason, there has been no similar uproar about their decline.

But first I must learn to identify them. With nine hundred resident species of macro moths, getting to know them is a testing task, not unlike the one that befalls the new schoolmaster on his first day. Take the pug family of moths – the one that causes the most problems of identification. There are 52 of them, brown and drab; they have as much charm as the litter you find in your trouser pocket after a bus journey. But identify them we must, like a schoolmaster, again, being presented with dull children and high fliers – they all need our attention. We cannot just study the exotic like the Mother Shipton (whose strange wing markings resemble a caricature of an old hag in profile, with conspicuous eye and hooked nose) nor just the handful of hawkmoths the size of small birds.

Mother Shipton

Then there is the fascinating Peppered Moth, described in the news as 'Darwin's Moth', a proof of natural selection because it is changing from its black form, from industrial pollution, back to its original white colour. I trapped a white one the other day. Not a trace of black thanks to the Clean Air Act.

Believe it or not there are species of moth called 'Uncertain' and 'Confused'. As if that isn't unscientific, the next two species could come from the imagination of Edward Lear: as my handbook says, 'The Brown-line Bright-eye is not to be confused with the Bright-line Brown-eye.'

With Mary urging me to attend to business, the prospect of identifying a hundred different moth species per day is daunting. It leaves little time for paid work...

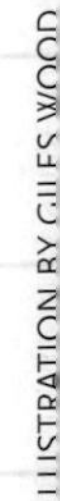

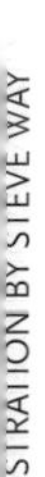
ILLUSTRATION BY STEVE WAY

My name is Michael Peterson

What does WILFRED DE'ATH *have in common with Britain's most dangerous criminal?*

MY OWN PRISON path and that of 'Charles Bronson', Britain's most violent criminal, crossed just once, in 1991, at the old Oxford jail (it is now student accommodation) where I was being held on remand and 'Bronson' was being transferred elsewhere because the screws couldn't handle him. A few of us cons watched in awe as he systematically trashed the reception area, doing several thousand pounds' worth of damage in about five minutes. A tiny bit of me, I don't mind admitting, was cheering him on...

I have put Bronson between inverted commas because his real name was (and is) Michael Peterson, a suburban nobody who set out to become 'somebody' via violent criminal activity in and out of jail. His career began with the botched armed robbery of a post office in 1974, since when he has spent 34 years in prison, many of them in solitary confinement. He remains in prison today.

I find Peterson's determination and persistence impressive. His intransigence, his pitting himself against the world ('I am the master of my fate, I am the captain of my soul') is, to some extent, reflected in my own escape from a colourless suburban background. Anyone who grew up, as I did, in horrible, boring places like Boreham Wood, Potters Bar and New Barnet should go to any lengths, up to and including mass murder, to avoid having to go back to them.

I once tried to explain to a callow young (female) probation officer, who seemed intent on discovering the basis for my deviance, that it was partly a search for identity and fame, that I was determined to be admitted to Madame Tussaud's and, if that meant inclusion in the Chamber of Horrors downstairs, rather than upstairs, well, so be it. I think the same might be said of Peterson, 'an unaccommodated and unaccommodating man', who is more at home in the nightmare world of bars, cages and strait-jackets than he would be in a suburban semi with a wife and kids. (Although there is a significant omission from the existential film and book about 'Bronson', and that is any discussion of the soul-destroying effects of long incarceration. Speaking only for myself, I know I couldn't handle it, which is why I have opted for life 'on the out'.)

There is one other way out: art. Peterson, as I insist he should be called, has developed considerable gifts as a writer and painter, winning many prizes.

My deviance was partly a search for identity and fame. The same might be said of Peterson

I suspect that, like myself, he possesses all the symptoms of genius without the disease; all the same, he has earned the right to be proud of his achievements, just as I am proud of my notoriety as a subversive journalist and surreal (amateur) artist. He has made a final, magnificent, defiant gesture of recalcitrance by smashing up the prison art studio, so he has gone one further than me. To catch him up, I shall have to set fire to the *Oldie* office. Watch this space!

RANT

ONE OF the minor hazards of Olden Life was treading in dogs' messes. In those days the streets of our towns and suburbs were littered with dogs' messes in various stages of freshness, and they were usually trodden on by children who didn't look where they were going or adults making their way home in the dark. Bringing a dog's mess home on one's shoe was greeted with a terrible cry of revulsion and despair: suspects were told to stay exactly where they were and advance no further into the house, after which they were expected to stand, stork-like, on one foot and then another so that the soles of their shoes could be inspected. Removing the mess was a repulsive business, still more so if tractor-soled shoes were involved, and the shoes were eventually propped up to dry after being thoroughly scrubbed with Jeyes Fluid.

Persuading dog owners to clear up behind them is, needless to say, an American innovation, but it has come at a price. Modern dog-owners are expected to grab hold of the mess in a polythene bag which they then turn inside-out and knot at one end before dropping it into a bin marked 'Dog Waste', many of which carry a comical silhouette of an Airedale standing over a steaming mess scored out with a large red cross. The trouble is that many dog-owners are too lazy or too stupid to carry the exercise through to its conclusion: they pick up the mess and put it in the bag but then hurl the thing on the ground. The result is the indestructible dog's mess. Richmond Park, the towpath of the Thames and even the South Downs are now peppered with polythene-wrapped dogs' messes, some of which have been there, to my certain knowledge, for three or four years at least. Left to its own devices, excrement will dry out in the sun or be washed away by the rain in a matter of days: these new horrors seem set to outlive us all. It makes me quite nostalgic for the bad old days.

JEREMY LEWIS

ILLUSTRATION BY TOM PLANT

Vengeance is mine...

Today's schoolchildren are protected from corporal punishment by law, but for most oldies it was part and parcel of school life – as was the inevitable encounter with a sadistic teacher. JOSEPH HONE *looks back on his own Wackford Squeers, sixty years on...*

Illustrated by Robert Geary

When Mr Dudgeon became headmaster of my boarding school in Dublin in the late 1940s, it might have seemed to an outsider that he was doing no more than pulling the place together, sharpening things up in a school where things had become a little lax. A school inspector would have commended his efforts. The purposes of education demanded no less. Why was it then that his arrival created such horror among us all, especially among a group of recently arrived senior boys?

It might have seemed to an outsider that he was merely pulling the place together...

The reason was simple. Dudgeon – unmarried, grey-haired, waxy-faced, fanatically neat in everything – was a sadist in the classic mould. In his previous job as science master in another Dublin boarding school he had terrorised his class in a variety of then usual ways – beating them vigorously at the least excuse, pulling the hair on the nape of their necks – and in some less usual ways of psychological torture.

Eventually, as a result, some of the bigger, tougher boys at this school had taken matters into their own hands. They had kidnapped Dudgeon, trussed him in a sack, put him in the back of a car, and driven him into the Dublin mountains, where they'd beaten him up, daubed him in red paint and left him to walk back in the middle of the night.

These half-dozen boys had immediately left the school and moved, most of them, to my school on the other side of town – then run by a kindly distinguished head (he'd played cricket with Sam Beckett for the Gentlemen of Ireland). Unfortunately, this man, Mr Cordiner, suffered an unexpected heart attack and died at the end of the summer term, soon after these boys arrived. During the holidays the Governors replaced Mr Cordiner – appointing Mr Dudgeon, of all people, instead.

So it was in that first assembly of the new term that we were confronted by Mr Dudgeon, this ogre, rubbing his hands briskly, eyeing us all carefully, particularly the boys who had beaten him up six months before. An astonishing moment – since it was clear to these boys, and to us others who had learnt of Dudgeon's reputation meanwhile, what was going to happen.

There followed a reign of terror in the school, in which Dudgeon, seeking revenge, took it out in any number of ways against the perpetrators of his original indignity and the other boys generally. The school became an occupied country, and the pupils, collaborators, resisters or refugees. Dudgeon, apart from his overt cruelties, was a subtle Cardinal straight out of the Inquisition. He presented a permanent and awful threat, seen or unseen. He had a quality of really sinister omnipresence. Absent from his sight, you knew he was looking for you; any close encounter meant you were about to be beaten. Like many such sadists of the old school, he gave a religious twist to his punishments. He once said to me, about to be beaten, 'Behold, I am with you always, Hone, even unto the end of the world.'

He had the awful gifts of a skilled police interrogator – convincing you that your best friend had told all an hour before and you were only there to confirm it

He had the awful gifts of a skilled police interrogator – convincing you that your best friend had told all an hour before and you were only there to confirm it. He played one boy off against another, placing informers and bribing potential fifth columnists, like a master spy running a network – a situation in which most of us became adept in the art of concealment and counter-terrorism.

Again, as in Dudgeon's previous school, it was some of the senior boys themselves who eventually took matters into their own hands.

Dudgeon continued to teach science in a wooden laboratory building some way from the main school. This was his other cruel domain, beyond his study, a sort of outlying Gestapo post, where he often went after dark to set up experiments for class next day. And it was here one evening that he was suddenly confronted by another half dozen senior boys, including some from the original raiding party.

Dudgeon knew what was afoot at once. He tried to laugh it off, in his usual cynical manner. 'Boys, nothing rash – I advise you clearly – it will be a matter for the police this time.' Dudgeon was cornered behind the long top desk. One of the boys opened a bottle of pure alcohol, spilling it all along the work-top, stood back and lit a match. 'I think – rather than the police – you will resign.' The boy then took out a cigarette and lit it with the match, puffing at it casually, gazing at Dudgeon. 'We're all leaving in a few days, end of school for us. And of course – the lab, it's all made of wood. And only one door, locked, of course, on the outside – with you inside. A bad fire. An accident, an unfortunate chemical reaction, a bottle of pure alcohol spilt by mistake. All common enough. Could happen at any time, couldn't it? Now – or next term. Or the one after,' the boy added pointedly, lighting another match and playing with it in the air.

Dudgeon capitulated – though only temporarily, as it turned out. But a year later, after we'd all left, the lab was burnt to the ground in mysterious circumstances. And Dudgeon did resign then, taking up the headmastership of an English public school, where no doubt his methods were found more acceptable. In any case, as far as our school was concerned, it was clear that the boys had kept their promise.

Paddy Chicken

When **DIARMAID Ó MUIRITHE** *arrived in a Limerick hamlet at midnight he was given a warm welcome by an enormous old man with an interesting past*

We arrived by taxi in the tiny hamlet of Barna, Co. Limerick, at midnight in the late autumn of 1957. Late as the hour was, we were greeted at the teacher's house we were to live in for the next few years by an enormous old man who had waited up and had a fire burning brightly in the hearth to welcome the three of us – my wife, our one-year-old son, and myself.

He ordered us to sit while he brought out a freshly made salad and a loaf of delicious soda bread. He refused to allow my wife to make the tea, and departed to the kitchen. He accepted our invitation to eat with us, and introduced himself as Paddy Ryan, and said that he was sometimes called Paddy Chicken, because of his frail disposition. This without a smile: he was about eighteen stone and six-foot-four when in his prime. He apologised for the 'excuse for a meal', blaming his wife, who had to visit a sick relative. Before he left, he put his hand in a coat pocket and produced a bottle of whiskey. He departed for the kitchen again and made punch for us. In answer to my question as to who he was and why he treated the new schoolmaster with such kindness, he said he was a neighbour. He insisted on leaving the whiskey when he left.

Gifted with a wonderful physique, and, it was said, as agile as a ballet dancer, he established a world record in the event which stood for twenty years

A great 'neighbour' (he actually lived a few miles away) he and his wife continued to be. The following day the local teacher, Jerry O'Sullivan, who had given him the key to our house as he had to go away on business, told me who he was.

He was born locally in 1887, and like many an Irishman of his day he emigrated to New York, where he worked as a builder's foreman and took up the sport of hammer throwing. Gifted with a wonderful physique, and, it was said, as agile as a ballet dancer, he established a world record in the event (189 feet 6 inches) which stood for twenty years, and as an American record until 1953. He won the American title every year between 1913 and 1921, apart from 1918 when he was in Europe with the US forces. But his greatest day came in 1920 at the Olympic Games in Antwerp, where at the age of 37, he was up against the Swedish favourite, Carl Lindt. His exploits that day make one of the great stories in Olympic history. I heard it from his own lips in Pallas-green, and he also related it to my journalist friend Brendan O'Reilly of Irish television. The truth of his version had earlier been confirmed by someone who witnessed the events, the American coach, Lawson Robertson, and by the American journalist Bill Dooley.

On the morning of the event Robertson was greeted by Ryan with the news that he was dying. He had imbibed a large quantity of French wine the night before which had given him a monumental hangover. Robertson panicked and went to get him. The Irishman seemed 'fairly all right' and was busy shaving and showering. After he was duly admonished, Ryan and his room-mate and best friend, the sculler John Kelly (later to become the father of a famous girl called Grace), set off for the stadium, but decided to break the journey on the way for a 'cure'. Ryan arrived late, having hitched a lift on the back of a lorry.

He was just in time. He found himself in the middle of a flaming row. His friend, the British hammer thrower Tom Nicolson, arrived late for the preliminary throws, and was told he was not going to be allowed to compete. Ryan created such a shindig, mentioning the war and Belgian ingratitude, that the decision against Nicolson's participation was reversed.

The other competitors had already taken their preliminary throws and Ryan saw the Swede's longest throw flagged in the distance. Then he noticed that he had left his official American team gear in the pub. Luckily, having small feet for such a big man, he was found a pair of spikes which fitted him.

His turn to throw came. There were muted objections to him throwing in his street clothes, but the British team, in a quid pro quo, voted with the Americans to allow him to compete. He must have looked a sight as, decked out in his shirt and trousers, and wearing a cloth cap, he squinted at the Swede's mark in the distance. He had one last request. He browbeat a young Belgian official into standing behind

Patrick Ryan, the Irish-born hammer thrower who took the gold medal for the USA in the 1920 Antwerp Olympics

PHOTOGRAPHY COURTESY OF © POPPERFOTO/GETTY IMAGES

'It was that last burger that did for him'

Carl Lindt's mark. 'I can't see the bloody thing,' he explained.

He pulled down his braces and threw away the cap. Then he whirled like the proverbial dervish and the Olympic official threw himself to the ground as the ball soared over his head to land fourteen feet seven inches beyond Lindt's mark, a distance which has stood as the greatest winning throw in Olympic history. He didn't bother to throw any more – he'd won by almost five yards. He also won a silver medal in the 56-lb throw in the same Olympics. They retrieved his gear in time for the presentation ceremony.

He returned to Ireland to run the little family farm in 1924. Walking home across the fields one night, he lost his medal. Half the parish looked in vain for it. Years later, a farmer ploughing a lea field saw something glittering as he turned the sod, bent down, and picked up his neighbour's Olympic treasure. Paddy, alas, had died in the meantime.

I went to his funeral in 1964 and saw the hammer with which he had broken the world record lying on his coffin. I remember fondly the kindly old giant who used to dandle my baby son John on his knee, looking with feigned contempt on me, a six-foot, twelve-stone weakling, and saying, 'No. How could he make a hammer thrower!' He made no secret of his disappointment that, while he fathered five lovely daughters, his pride and joy, he had no son.

How good was he? He told a modern great American gold medallist, Harold Connolly, who came to visit him, that he would have beaten him. Connolly looked at old Paddy sitting in his chimney corner, and answered: 'Yes, Mr Ryan, I think you might have, if you'd kept the hangovers to a minimum.'

THAT WAS THE SUMMER

by Kit Wright
Illustrated by Peter Bailey

That was the summer as I recall,
the man next door and I began
to call each other Sir,
in a kind of roguish formality or
mock-combative collusion. Why,
I cannot say, but keep it up
we somehow did for some little time;
for as long, you might almost say, as it took.
"Are you all right, sir?" "Quite all right, sir.
You all right, sir?" "Sir, I'm well."
Nor did we fail to operate
attendant quasi-theatrical business:
the stiff half-turn; the ritual bow;
the planted stare of profound regard,
as we met on our doorsteps, housekeys poised...
or bellowed across the howling High Road
"ARE YOU ALL RIGHT, SIR?" "QUITE ALL RIGHT, SIR!"
as though in loyal defence of a principle
both were prepared to die for, soon.
But the ending seemed as inexplicable
as the beginning: the disappearance,
ambulance sirens, police, old pressmen
hogging the bar at the Horse and Artichoke,
cats gone skinny, the dog marooned.
And of course I know no more than anyone
else as I walk these streets at midnight,
hoping to coax from neon or starlight
a final reflexive "Sir, I'm well".

Modern life

'We have to get ourselves a stronger coffee table'

What is... Compliance?

ORIGINALLY WE hoped the outbreak could be confined to two filthy old pigs called Jonathan and Russell, and few of us foresaw the terrible power of the thing unleashed in October 2008. Now, no power on earth can stop Compliance from spreading into every sinew and nerve of the BBC.

The symptoms are mild at first – a bit of arse-covering here and there – but resistance is futile, and before you know it you'll be referring up and passing the buck on a daily basis. It was all triggered by Ross and Brand's deeply unfunny persecution of Andrew Sachs, but in reaching for Compliance to prevent such cock-ups in the future, the BBC has grasped not a cure but a deadly disease.

Like many public bodies, the BBC is bound by the rules of quangos such as Ofcom and the Health and Safety Executive, as well the editorial guidelines and rules of governance laid down by its own Charter. By feeding obsessively on these pettifogging regulations, Compliance lays low its victim, robs it of its own judgement and creativity and forces it to comply at all times, treating mere guidelines as cast-iron laws, however bovine, politically correct and restrictive this may be.

Hang on – you mean to say Compliance is just about complying with everything? That sounds like our friend 'Stating the Bleedin' Obvious' up to his old tricks again. Well, yes and no. Compliance has worked as a low-level infection in the BBC for years. For example, the Corporation has long been taken for a ride by so-called security consultants: you cannot be sent off to report a war or a terrorist attack unless you have completed your Hostile Environments course (three days of running around a spinney being throttled during mock kidnaps by psychotic ex-paratroopers). Naturally, that won't qualify you for a riot. For that you must attend the Riot Awareness course. And even when you get to your war you have to consult the meddlers in the BBC High Risk Team or Special Events Team, usually made up of bossy ex-coppers and passed-over army captains called Ralph.

But now, thanks to the severe outbreak of Compliance, the rise of the desk-bound BBC busybody is inexorable. The

Resistance is futile, and before you know it you'll be referring up and passing the buck on a daily basis

place is teeming with 'Compliance Officers' whose numbers include refugees from the equality departments of incompetent, politically correct Labour councils, and over-promoted clerks who claim to understand the Data Protection Act. These people police the BBC on behalf of outside bodies to ensure it adheres to their rules. We now have the 'Information Policy and Compliance Team' and, to really rub it in, a 'Compliance Unit'. The 'Compliance Portal' has made an appearance on the internal website and the 'Pan-BBC Compliance Framework' makes clear the 'paramount importance of Compliance', warning darkly about the consequences of non-compliance: 'There may also be financial penalties and, in certain circumstances, financial liability.'

The trigger for a deadly disease: Russell Brand (left) and Jonathan Ross in the programme which caused offence in October 2008

Compliance is fuelled by fear – the fear of taking a decision, or acting in a way which in some way displeases Compliance. Practically everyone is terrified of making a decision about anything without consulting one of the Compliance Stasi because the word 'no' is the cough made by Compliance – no, you can't go there; no, you can't say that – and Compliance demands obeisance to regulations which are just a long-winded way of saying 'no'. A few years ago, I remember a fellow news correspondent agreeing with his editor about the number of swear words he could use in a radio piece – one b*stard, two f**ks and no c**ts. Today, he would have to go over the head of his editor to the Head of Compliance who would say 'no'. 'Yes' is a risky business and hardly ever complies.

Naturally, senior managers love Compliance because it protects them from taking any responsibility for the actions of staff. With Compliance, blame is clearly set out and safely apportioned to the disposable underling, enshrining in black and white the old BBC maxim of 'deputy heads must roll'. What might have been quite useful in moderation is now just institutionalised timidity. Compliance allows ineffective leaders like BBC Director General Mark Thompson to manage processes rather than people and avoid any risk to the pension pot. Perhaps the BBC should change its motto, 'Nation shall speak peace unto nation.' Somehow, 'Comply or die' feels more appropriate and would sound even better in Latin.

NORMAN DEPLUME

Olden life

What was... a British Warm?

DURING THE First World War, dissatisfaction with military equipment led to the design of a British Warm. This item of menswear was based on the army greatcoat issued to officers in the Great War, as specified in the bizarre language of the depot storekeeper – 'overcoat, British, warm, officers of field rank for the use of.' It was itself a well-respected 'piece of kit', evidenced in Rudyard Kipling's story 'The Debt' in which an old Indian servant makes the admiring, albeit mispronounced, comment, 'Yes, all the world knows *Baritish warrum*'. The difference between the two pieces of uniform was essentially in the length. The problem with the greatcoat was that the hem was low enough to absorb substantial quantities of the mud and water of the trenches on the front line. What was needed was a shorter coat.

As a private purchase, trimmed to thigh length, it became so popular that it soon featured in regimental dress regulations, and was approved as officers' dress in the *Guidance to Young Officers Handbook*. It also found favour on the dress list for officers and Warrant Officers (Class 1) of the Household Cavalry, with the caveats of 'No badges of rank' and 'Not to be worn on Parade'.

The dictionary definition is 'a double-breasted overcoat of military cut.' More specifically, a tailor's description, to differentiate it from other overcoats, is 'six-button double-breasted topcoat, peak lapels, welt breast pocket, slanting lower flap pockets, epaulettes, slightly shaped body lines'. The usual material was a taupe-coloured Melton cloth. Originating from Melton Mowbray, it is described by the celebrated tailor Leonard Logsdail, and echoed by Anderson & Sheppard Bespoke Tailors of Old Burlington Street, as 'thick, tightly woven napped cloth, first woven for riding and hunting garments. The authentic Melton cloth weighs in at 34 oz.'

Not only was it a favourite item of attire with officers 'in mufti' through the two world wars, but its smart lines made it attractive to businessmen and civil servants alike. Some of the most popular public figures have been photographed wearing a British Warm – Churchill meeting Roosevelt at Yalta in 1945, for instance.

After World War Two, the coat was put to use by dodgy characters, acquiring slightly 'spivvy' connotations

What then caused the British Warm to be deserted by its once-loyal followers? The answer is that after World War Two the coat was put to use by dodgy characters, acquiring slightly 'spivvy' connotations of the black market and car dealers in Warren Street.

Moreover, as is so often the case, public perception was reinforced by what was seen on the cinema or television, and for every Clive Candy 'good egg' we find cads and bounders in the characters of Major Courtney (Cecil Parker) in *The Ladykillers*, Major Hitchcock (Terry-Thomas) in *I'm All Right Jack*, and Rigsby (Leonard Rossiter) playing the gentleman in an episode of *Rising Damp* – 'Pink Carnations'.

Above: A British Warm, as illustrated in an advertisement from 1918
Below: Cecil Parker in *The Ladykillers* wearing a British Warm coat

Soon the British Warm lost sales in favour of 'civilian' cut overcoats and was consigned to the back of the wardrobe, perhaps to see the light of day once a year on Remembrance Sunday.

So, as a private purchaser without benefit of the mess tailor, is it still possible to buy a British Warm?

Well, certainly not in any high-street gents outfitters or the menswear departments of the large chain stores. You will search in vain for an off-the-peg stockist in this country. No, it would be necessary to have it made-to-measure by a traditional bespoke tailor, always providing the pattern is still on file – otherwise 'you will have to bring a picture'. Enquiries at No. 1 Savile Row reveal that although it is no longer a Gieves & Hawkes stock item, their military branch will be pleased to make an appointment to take your measurements for a British Warm – a snip at £900 and a making-up time of eight weeks.

The sun may have finally set on this charismatic topcoat in its native country, just another casualty of the relentless forces of fashion, but 'somewheres east of Suez' a British Warm is still on parade.

JOHN GRANT GIBSON

Alec Bedser

In 2009 **ROBERT CHESSHYRE** *talked to one of the greatest English cricketers of the twentieth century. This 'Still With Us' piece first appeared in The Oldie in April 2009*

There is a joke in cricket circles that Sir Alec Bedser was the second English 'bowler' to be knighted. The first was Sir Francis Drake, who famously refused to allow his game on Plymouth Hoe to be interrupted by the Armada. Sir Francis – 'Captain, art thou sleeping there below?' – is, of course, centuries gone, while Sir Alec, who will be 91 on July 4th 2009, is, happily, very much still with us, living quietly outside Woking in his cricketing county of Surrey.

He greets me on a sunny winter's morning. His left knee is painfully arthritic and he uses a stick and a stair-lift, but he still drives, looks after himself and has a memory as sharp as a tack. Since the death of his twin brother and fellow cricketer Eric, he has lived in the house that his father, a bricklayer, built (with the twins' help) for the family in 1952. Players with diamond studs in their noses, highlights in their hair and Ferraris in the garage seem light-years away.

The Australian cricketers arrive this summer for an 'Ashes' series, provoking no doubt many replays of 2005, when Andrew Flintoff and team defeated the Aussies to lift the most famous prize in the summer game. We will be shown those tearful and alcoholically emotional scenes as the players – bottles in hand – toured Trafalgar Square in an open-top bus. Later the whole team received gongs.

Bedser snorts. 'Fancy getting het up like that: a disgrace, wasn't it, getting drunk? We won the Ashes at the Oval in 1953, and we didn't celebrate at all. We went to the Australian dressing room – they were all mates – and had a couple of beers, and then I caught the train to Woking. I was playing for Surrey two days later.' It was largely due to Bedser that England triumphed – a fast-medium pace bowler of metronomic accuracy, he took 39 wickets at an average of 17.48 per wicket in the series, with a two innings analysis of 14 for 99 at Trent Bridge.

He views short forms of the game, especially Twenty20, with distaste

Players received £65 per match, less the fees they would have been paid by their counties, giving Bedser a net £42. He still remembers warmly a *Sunday Express* writer who paid him five pounds for a quote. In winter, when there was no England tour, he and Eric had to take what work they could find. He spent one winter digging trees in a garden nursery: he was then one of the best-known sportsmen in England.

Bedser, made as it were of English oak, only left the field once in over fifty Test matches – and then briefly when the Adelaide temperature soared. The day we meet, there is news that Flintoff, playing in the Caribbean, had been flown 500 miles for a scan on a side strain. Another snort. 'I played many a time with a pain,' says Bedser, who puts down his fitness to digging in allotments. Between April 1946 and September 1947, he bowled 3,000 overs – and went to Australia and back by sea. Today England players are ordered to take it easy between Test matches.

He developed a fast leg-cutter, with which he dismissed the peerless Don Bradman for a duck – 'the best ball that ever got me out,' acknowledged the Don. Bedser believes he is the only Test bowler to dismiss Bradman twice for nought, and in all took his wicket five times in six matches. Bedser asks me to fetch a commemorative ball from his mantelpiece, and in his huge right hand shows me how he learned to grip the ball across the seam to achieve the cutter.

Bedser left school at fourteen; worked for a solicitor, quitting when an ex-public schoolboy received a higher pay rise. Never having played cricket on grass until he was fifteen nor held a new ball until he was seventeen, nonetheless he and Eric were taken on the Surrey playing staff in 1938 – 'I never had any idea that I would be any good.' In his case, the Germans, rather than the Armada, rudely interrupted his bowling: he and Eric, then RAF police, were strafed by a bomber – 'the bullets went between us.'

He was demobbed in March 1946, and by mid-summer was playing for England, taking 22 wickets in his first two Test matches. He had not touched a bat or ball for two-and-a-half years. Today a month out of the game is considered a fair enough excuse for loss of form. Bedser never bowled a bouncer – 'waste of energy' – and his wicket-keepers always stood up to the stumps.

He retired from Test cricket in 1955, with a then record of 236 wickets, and became

COLOUR PORTRAIT BY JEFF GILBERT, BLACK AND WHITE COURTESY OF GETTY IMAGES the longest-serving selector, chairman, and occasional tour manager. There was no medal for his Ashes heroics in 1953, but eventually reward for his services came by way of an OBE, a CBE and finally – in 1997 – his knighthood. Don Bradman, a lifelong friend, wrote that, wonderful though the honour was, a man still needed three meals a day. Such down-to-earth philosophy has always guided Bedser.

He views short forms of the game – especially Twenty20, which he dismisses as 'baseball' – with distaste. Cricket skills are honed in the long game: 'If that goes, class and standards will fall: where are you going to produce cricketers?' He accepts that the game needs money, or talented players will seek careers elsewhere – 'you can't blame them for cashing in.' However, he is less sympathetic to the cult of celebrity. 'Rubbish, it is: people read the news and they call them "celebs".'

OPPOSITE: Alec Bedser in the garden at the house the Bedsers built
ABOVE: Derbyshire's Bert Alderman bowled by Alec Bedser at the Oval, 25 July 1947

Eric, the older twin by ten minutes, was never picked for England, but had a successful career with Surrey. He died in 2006, leaving Alec alone in the Woking house. 'People don't understand how close we were: we shared money; we shared everything.' They dressed alike – 'if we wanted a suit, we might as well get two.' Neither married: their closeness must have unnerved women. In any case, the constant travelling meant that top players' marriages were often difficult.

I leave Sir Alec to his simple lunch of pork pie and salad, eaten while he reads the *Daily Telegraph*. 'I hope you've got enough guff for your piece,' he says.

• *Alec Bedser died on 4 April 2010*

NOT MANY DEAD

Important stories you may have missed

Rock singer Pete Doherty stunned locals at The Dundas Arms, Kintbury, when he strolled in for supper on Monday night.
Newbury Weekly News

Plans to open a new Iceland store in Hailsham town centre are still being finalised.
Sussex Express

Sheppey Coastguard was called to the naturist beach at Leysdown following a report of a dog in the water, but nothing untoward was found.
Sheerness Times Guardian

The Queen cut a cake in celebration of the 250th anniversary of the Royal Botanic Gardens at Kew yesterday, with a little help from the Duke of Edinburgh.
Daily Telegraph

A new ticket office has been opened at Euston pending upgrade work at the terminus. It is located behind the former ticket office.
The Railway Magazine

Park café has a run on ice creams.
Newbury Weekly News

A small fire in a toaster was out when firefighters arrived at a bungalow at Windmill Platt, Handcross.
West Sussex County Times

Jordan found some unfinished songs left behind by husband Peter Andre at their home. 'I have not bothered to listen to them,' she admits.
Metro

Sick people have been blamed for Colchester General Hospital failing to meet its targets.
The Gazette

Motorists face a clear journey home this evening.
thisisderbyshire.co.uk

A man accused of having caused criminal damage to two beef burgers walked free from Swansea Magistrates Court after the charge was dropped. Stephen Morgan, 31, rejected the burgers after they were delivered late.
The Times

A tin of Spam was stolen when thieves broke into a canal boat in Barnacre.
Garstang Courier

A cat whose meow sounds like Jimmy Savile's catchphrase 'Now then, now then' has gone missing in Romford, Essex.
The Sun

Clyde *and the* Diva

Fancy a diversion? Tempted to look up an old, possibly now-famous admirer? Retired opera singer **ANNE HOWELLS** *would advise you to be careful what you wish for...*

Illustrated by **MARTIN HONEYSETT**

The Diva had spent many years on the circuit as a jobbing operatic soprano. There had been (brief) moments of glory – like having her birthday revealed once a year in the *Times* and the *Telegraph* alongside Bruce Forsyth and Muhammad Ali, and glamorous receptions such as a never-to-be-forgotten night in Brussels when, asked by the Belgian Prime Minister's wife if her gown was Balenciaga, she replied, 'No, Pauline of Cockfosters'.

At the beginning of her career and while under contract to a major opera house, she had appeared with the Oxbridge Operatic Society as a nymph in Richard Strauss's *Ariadne auf Naxos*, a part which gave her plenty of time backstage, where she got to know a duffel-coated student called Clyde, who was appearing in a short operatic work in the same programme. The Diva was then in her twenties, as slim as a reed and with shoulder-length red hair, and it soon became apparent that Clyde was nursing a passion for her.

Many years later, in 2005, the Diva turned round and discovered that everybody had died. Up to her neck in the unmentionable doings of those around her (these are enshrined in a novel which has been cleared for libel at great expense) she had had to cope with more slings and arrows than should have been her share. One night when it was raining and all there was to watch on TV was *Do I Ever Have News That Is Actually New?* she saw Clyde, who in the interim had found fame and fortune as a distinguished writer and critic (it may come as a surprise to his admirers that he should have appeared in an opera).

She decided to write to him to say hello. To her delight and surprise, he invited her to dinner *chez lui* in his Docklands pad. After a couple of bottles of wine Clyde peered at her over the table. 'Be my mistress,' he suggested. The Diva considered. She had retired from the circuit by now and the new plasma television with its aerial facing Midhurst had turned out to be a big disappointment. When it rained she could only get BBC One.

As she stood next to his bed she hoped he would recognise quality when he saw it. He opened his eyes and looked at her. 'I've been eating shortbread,' he informed her, 'so you can start by sucking the crumbs from between my teeth'

'Is there a vacancy then?' she now enquired, and Clyde said that there was. 'All right,' she said. 'I'll give it a go.'

'Shake on it?' suggested Clyde, holding out his hand, and they did exactly that.

Surprisingly, the Diva was not quite sure as to what being a mistress entailed, but gamely lashed out on a *devoré* velvet negligée from Fortnum and Mason's in which to blunder around Clyde's apartment (he seemed to have a thing about switching on the lights). As she stood next to his bed she hoped that he would recognise quality when he saw it. He opened his eyes and looked at her. 'I've been eating shortbread,' he informed her, 'so you can start by sucking the crumbs from between my teeth.'

When the Diva had recovered from the feelings that this invitation induced and had ascertained that there was no medicinal brandy to hand, the two got down to talking about the arias and songs that Clyde had in his operatic repertoire. The Diva was stunned. '"Nessun' dorma?"' she asked disbelievingly. 'Ernesto's aria from *Don Pasquale*? Berlioz' "Nuits d'Eté"? Do you actually sing these, Clyde?'

He airily replied that his singing teacher had 'put two octaves' on his voice and that he was now a dramatic tenor. As most singers are happy to have two and a half octaves to start or even finish up with, the addition of another two octaves to his voice must surely have put Clyde in the running to sing the stratospheric roulades of the Queen of the Night.

Anxious to demonstrate his new skills, Clyde embarked on a rendition of a Fauré chanson. Half a page in, the Diva spotted French through the Australian and wished she had had a hankie to stuff in her mouth. Clyde was miffed when she criticised his accent, and anyway had ideas about substituting hankie-pankie for the hankie. This last activity was usually accompanied by a sort of running commentary by Clyde as if a camera were mounted on a track running the length of the bedroom. The Diva often felt that a voice might shout 'cut'.

The Diva's criticism of Clyde's French obviously rankled, and he had ideas for improvement. 'Tell you what,' he said over tea one afternoon. 'You can give me French lessons – I'll pay you twenty quid an hour.' 'Stick a nought on the end of that,' replied the Diva, who was tiring of the bedroom documentaries and beginning to welcome any diversion, 'and we might be in business.'

As the 'affair' progressed, the Diva perceived more and more that being Clyde's mistress was losing its appeal. Eventually Clyde summoned the Diva to his pad on a gloomy December afternoon. As usual there were no lights on, but she managed to make out his face through the gloaming. There was something in the air and it was not just smoke from the burning Christmas pudding that he had elected to serve with afternoon tea. In a while, with a mouthful of pud and brandy sauce, he disclosed through a hail of dried fruit that he could 'Berlioz' no more. He did not make clear if this sudden inability was through disinclination or indisposition but his reasons were long-winded and abstruse, and the Diva lost interest half-way through.

Happily, the Diva has moved on to a partner whose grasp of Berlioz is remarkable and who does not talk with his mouth full. He also has a knack with aerials and the Diva is now able to receive several channels all at once and in glorious definition.

'In the book they just hold hands'

Flights of *fancy*

As the former political editor for Channel 4, **ELINOR GOODMAN** *flew around the globe with various prime ministers on the hunt for a story...*

They were the best of trips and the worst of trips – travelling with different prime ministers as they flew round the globe visiting other world leaders. The political hacks were bottled in the back of a VC10 in great comfort, the Prime Minister and the Downing Street entourage sat in the front. Food and drink were served from the moment you got on board. You didn't even have to sit down when the plane took off.

Every now and then Alastair Campbell, or whoever was the Prime Minister's spokesman at the time, would come back to try and make the most of a captive press corps. But, desperate to justify the huge expense of sending us on the trip, we would usually agree among ourselves a better story than the one being offered. In the vacuum-packed atmosphere of the cabin, stories bred like germs. It was when Alastair Campbell was still political editor of the *Daily Mirror* that he managed to persuade the rest of the flying pack that he had distinctly seen John Major's shirt tucked into his underpants. From that flight a myth was born.

I never understood why prime ministers came back to the press cabin. It was started by Mrs Thatcher, but in those days the pack was far friendlier. I am embarrassed to say that we serenaded her, with a *Sun* wordsmith writing a song for each trip. The song was usually a bit risqué but, not surprisingly, she loved it, and it did wonders for her relations with the press.

Despite having witnessed so many of John Major's unhappy jousts with

ILLUSTRATION BY BOB GEARY

journalists on the plane, Alastair Campbell duly escorted Tony Blair down the gangway. Blair would often complain that his words had been taken out of context, and vow never to come back again. But he needed us as much as we needed him. I remember once being woken by Tony Blair standing above me – I was stretched out across four seats – and wondering why on earth he didn't try to sleep himself.

We went to some wonderful places – South Africa, and, of course, the Azores for Blair's 2003 summit with George W Bush. My main preoccupation was not the rights and wrongs of the imminent war with Iraq but how to get across a field of cows to where I was supposed to do a piece to camera. For a television journalist, logistics are everything. You arrive at a destination, help the crew gather up their gear, then drive like the clappers to get to where the prime minister is. There would then be a few minutes for a bit of filming, followed by several hours of hanging around for a press conference. The press would then get on their phones and file their copy. But we had to edit a piece for television, which takes much longer. Sometimes we would go to the local television stations – in Saudi Arabia I remember recording a piece under a plastic palm tree. On other occasions we huddled in the backs of vans or slumped on beds in hotel rooms. It was always a rush to get on the plane. The press corps would already be on their second glass of champagne as we hurtled up the steps.

One of the most exotic trips with Blair was to Libya to see President Gaddafi in May 2007. We were driven out into the desert where he had set up his tent. The centre of Libyan government is always where the President's tent has been pitched, and it was apparently moved even as we were arriving at the airport. But nobody had told our bus driver, so after speeding along for half an hour, he suddenly screeched to a U-turn and set off in the opposite direction.

Gaddafi had brought along his camels to show Tony Blair, though Blair didn't seem very interested in them, and the camels showed a haughty disdain for all of us. The two leaders sat in the tent in full view of the cameras, supposedly negotiating. But most of the real work had almost certainly been done by officials. Rather than listening to Blair, Gaddafi seemed more interested in us – political editors struggling to record pieces to camera in front of the tent against a background noise of camels burping. All this without over-running our allotted three minutes of satellite time.

I went to places I would never otherwise have visited. I nearly got left behind in the spectacularly beautiful Umayyad Mosque in Damascus because the Prime Minister's motorcade moved off through the *souq* without me. I saw leaders like Nelson Mandela in the flesh. But I am ashamed to say that I found the trips very stressful – partly because they were so expensive. I felt I should be giving Channel 4 something extra for its money. I had the added – and now, I realise, ridiculous – preoccupation with what I looked like. Nick Robinson didn't have enough hair to ruin it by sleeping on the plane. I was supposed to look presentable when I did the mandatory piece to camera in front of a landmark to prove that I had left Westminster and wasn't just voicing over somebody else's picture. I would borrow the flight attendant's Carmen rollers, while on the other side of the divide, Cherie's hairdresser gave her the full works.

There was also the worry that a colleague might come up with a scoop, or that the political editors of the Sunday papers would invent one of their own. As a result I would get horrific indigestion, burping like one of Gaddafi's camels, and be desperate for a decent night's sleep. But nowadays, strapped into economy class with my knees pressed against my chin and a howling child beside me, I do reflect on how times have changed. I now have more time to explore countries than on those trips when a long stay was a day. But I do miss the VIP departure lounge, and the chance of being in on the making of history.

Rather than listening to Blair, Gaddafi seemed more interested in us – political editors struggling to record pieces to camera with a background of burping camels

Is there a doctor on the bus?

Although **FRANCIS KING** *never fulfilled his childhood ambition to become a doctor, he still likes to act out the role whenever the opportunity arises*

Do children still play Doctors and Nurses? Probably not – unless in a computer version. That was my favourite game when I was six, and eighty years later I still continue to play it. When a visitor to my childhood home once asked me, 'What do you want to be when you grow up?', I replied, without a moment's hesitation, 'A doctor.' My father – perhaps because he had spent so much money on Swiss sanatoria in a futile attempt to be cured of the TB that eventually killed him at an early age – at once firmly intervened: 'Certainly not.' From this opposition he never deviated; and since paternal authority and filial piety were both far stronger then than now, I abandoned any thought of entering the medical profession but consoled myself by still secretly pretending to myself that I belonged to it.

One of my neighbours is, according to her own accounts, a prey to an astonishing variety of ailments. If another (male) neighbour happens to be chatting to me as she emerges from her house, he at once abandons me – 'Oh, God, there's that ghastly woman! I avoid her like the plague.' But I, in my doctor's role, am delighted to see her. I am fascinated by whatever is her symptom of the day, the more abstruse the better. I am flattered when she asks me 'Do you think it normal that I itch so much?'

I have now convinced myself that I have acquired the almost supernatural diagnostic powers once ascribed to Lord Horder, who within five minutes knew exactly what was wrong with a patient without all the elaborate and expensive tests now available to even the humblest of practitioners.

The way in which so many doctors today lack such diagnostic powers was confirmed for me when I visited a GP about an agonisingly swollen foot. 'I think I've got gout.' There was no thinking about it, I was sure. She examined the foot with evident distaste. 'That's not gout. That's cellulitis.' She then dashed off a prescription for an antibiotic. Eighteen months later I was back with the foot again agonisingly swollen. 'I'm afraid my cellulitis has returned.' 'That's not cellulitis. That's gout.' Her tone was the same withering one on both occasions.

Doctors rarely welcome self-diagnoses. Four years ago, having suddenly lost much of my peripheral vision, I took myself off to my nearest hospital. 'I have a detached retina,' I told the doctor. After he and a colleague had examined me, he said firmly: 'No, there's no sign of a detached retina. I'm afraid you must have had a stroke.' Then he asked in a far from friendly voice: 'Are you by any chance a medical journalist?' To my shame, my diagnostic intuition had for once failed me.

I am convinced that I have the almost supernatural diagnostic powers once ascribed to Lord Horder, who within five minutes knew exactly what was wrong

Not long ago I was travelling on a bus when suddenly a female passenger at the rear became violently ill. The bus-driver did not shout 'Is there a doctor on the bus?', but in a foreign accent pleaded, 'Can anyone please help?' I began to struggle to my feet when a young man announced, 'I'm a nurse,' jumped up and scuttled down the bus to the still vomiting woman. Meanwhile the bus-driver was telephoning for an ambulance and a bus replacement.

I felt a resentment towards this creature who had so brutally usurped my starring role in the drama. I was therefore not best pleased when he came across and stood beside me while we all waited at the bus-stop.

'I think that poor thing must have eaten something,' he said.

I shook my head 'No, I don't think so.' I did not attempt to conceal my scorn for his diagnosis. 'It's this norovirus that's been sweeping London. Projectile vomiting,' I added. 'The distinguishing symptom.'

'Yes, yes. That must be it, doctor. Of course.'

He now gazed at me with a new respect.

What a happy day, a day to be remembered! It was as though an actor known for his playing of the Gravedigger in *Hamlet* had suddenly been mistaken for a real-life gravedigger.

John Michell

9 February 1933 – 24 April 2009

CANDIDA LYCETT GREEN pays tribute to the philosopher, visionary, writer, artist, mystic, radical traditionalist and world authority on ancient science who was *The Oldie*'s 'Orthodox Voice' from the magazine's first issue in 1992 until his death in 2009

John was my friend for fifty years. More than anyone, he made me realise that it was arrogant not to believe in almost everything. As his pupil I subscribed to the *Flying Saucer Review* in the early 1960s: why shouldn't there be any other intelligence than our own?

John was the polar opposite of a sceptic. I admired his constant questioning and frequent disdain of received opinion and I found his passion for England, and for the obscure and unloved within it, inspiring and infectious. He embraced everyone – especially the fallen or broken – with a loving and gentle warmth. In 1966, he wrote me a list entitled 'Good Things'. It read: 'huge, sad people with ginger moustaches in saloon bars; Wing Commanders with their own beer mugs; people who say "Hello John, how's John?"; Salvation Army bands at Oxford; Accrington Stanley football team's laundress, Mrs Reg Gutteridge, packing up the shirts for the last time' (the team had just been disbanded).

John loved travelling by barge, the Isle of Man, old-school Notting Hill Gate society, small churches and chapels, village fêtes, tracks and green lanes, second-hand bookshops, private presses, debunking the pompous, Padstow Mayday, sacred sites, one-inch maps, and the Vicar of Morwenstow (included in his book *Eccentric Lives and Peculiar Notions*). He had an old Morris Minor which he never used on motorways, choosing instead to meander to his destination on small roads. Journeying with him was always an odyssey of magical discoveries – barrows hidden in woods, green men, Celtic crosses.

John was funny, never unkind, full of wonder and always enthusiastically bolstering about anything I was working on. Highly intelligent, he never took himself seriously and always kept an open mind. The usual sceptics closed theirs at the outset of the great crop-circle phenomenon in the 1990s. John knew that some of the circles were man-made, but there was room to believe that some were not. It was the consternation, awe and argument they engendered which delighted him and was reflected in his magazine, the *Cereologist*.

'Mr Michell – who incessantly rolled his own cigarettes, sometimes using tobacco – led the way in making Glastonbury an epicenter of New Age curiosities' (*New York Times* obituary)

I was always impressed by John's extraordinary (usually nocturnal) industry, particularly as he smoked dope full-time. Not only did he write myriad exhaustively researched books (*Megalithomania*, *The Earth Spirit*, *A Little History of Astro-Archaeology*, *Phenomena*, *Living Wonders*, *The View Over Atlantis*, to name a few), pamphlets, lectures and articles, all executed with a delicate, light and often witty touch, but he also painted many exquisite miniature watercolours. He fuelled and enriched the imagination of so many, especially the younger generation. Like Alfred Watkins's *The Old Straight Track*, which has been in print since 1929, so *The View Over Atlantis* will remain a seminal book among alternative society.

Two years ago, on the balmiest of days, we drove through pastoral Somerset to John's wedding in Glastonbury. England had never looked so beautiful. We took the small lanes between cow parsley waves which John loved, and zig-zagged around geometrical ditches towards the Tor, John's Mecca. Tall and willowy, he had seldom looked so elegant in his lightweight black and white check suit, standing outside St Benedict's among a merry throng. The guests were dressed in all the colours of the rainbow, some wearing wreaths of ivy, flowers and oak leaves. A horse-drawn gypsy carriage carried the couple along winding streets to the town hall, followed by a gaggle of children and the straggling guests. It was like a scene from Hardy or *A Midsummer Night's Dream*. (The marriage, his first, lasted no time at all.)

Two years later, the beauty of that scene was eclipsed. As though God had arranged it, at almost exactly the same time in early May, we drove to his funeral along ever narrower lanes through what the pastoral poet William Barnes, loved by John, described as 'deepenst Dorset'. John had died in the bosom of his son Jason's family. The sun shone while he was borne on a horse-drawn cart through the village to Stoke Abbot church, set in its idyllic bowl of small hills. He lies on a gentle slope of the churchyard now, sheep grazing in the valley which falls away beyond. You could call it paradise on earth.

MEMORY LANE

Every month Oldie readers take a trip down Memory Lane by describing what they were doing 30, 40, 50, 60, 70, 80 or even 90 years ago

40 years ago I was on board the Polaris submarine, HMS *Repulse*, for her first deterrent patrol. We had loaded the last of the Polaris missiles the previous night and slipped away before dawn. Even though most of our 7,500 tons was underwater, the submarine lifted and fell slowly in the Atlantic swell.

Diving is not dramatic; indicators click, but at first there is no other sign that the boat is submerging. Then I felt the deck tilt under my feet. The captain was the last to see the sky as the periscope was lowered. We dived to our operating depth and went silently to our patrol area.

The captain was the last to see the sky as the periscope was lowered. We would not see daylight again for 8 weeks

We would not see daylight again for eight weeks.

We settled into a routine. Our clocks stayed on GMT regardless of real time outside. The passage of time was marked by regular meal-times and dimmed lights to make night. The routine was four hours on watch in the control room and eight off. Every third night we got a full night of sleep when we were off watch from midnight till eight in the morning. On watch, we kept the boat silent and deep. We were able to receive messages from headquarters ashore, but we never transmitted. The chart table in the control room was a blank sheet of paper unmarked with latitude or longitude. There was just a rectangle, representing our patrol area. We wandered slowly and randomly across it.

Life on patrol was rather like being on a retreat: no radio, no television, no papers – but there was a movie each evening. Once a week we received a twenty-word 'family-gram'. It was a challenge for our wives to sum up family news in twenty words, but this was our only link to life ashore.

Our routine was broken at random intervals by an urgent message calling us to prepare to fire our missiles. The alarm went and we closed up to action stations. My task was to bring the boat up to firing depth and stop it on a dime. Indicator lights showed the readiness of the missiles, changing in stages from red to 16 green lights. We were ready inside the required 15 minutes.

The test over, we returned to our operational depth. Eventually, we got the signal that our relief boat was on station and we could go home. A night watch on the bridge was the first fresh air we had breathed and the first sky we had seen for two months.

David Higham

A Polaris submarine

90 years ago – yes, I am 95, but I remember very clearly the day when the big gate clanged shut and a strong man was sent to stand inside, frowning to stop anyone coming in or going out. Bubonic plague had hit Patna, India, and my father was going to prevent its creeping into our compound. Everybody was going about with a solemn face; even the Untouchable Woman, who used to tempt me into her hut with little armchairs and tables made out of bamboo bits for my dolls, had lost her toothless smile.

Ayah could not take me out for our usual walk that day. She was busy gossiping so I had been able to run away from her. I wanted to play with Ali, the gardener's son. He was a bit older than me and had lots of good ideas for exciting games such as teasing the monkeys in the wood behind the bungalow. We pelted them with pebbles to make them so mad with rage that they ran shrieking and chattering along the branches, leaping from tree to tree, and sometimes the biggest grand-father of the tribe leaned down and tried to grab our hair. So far we had always got away, laughing but a bit frightened too. But Ali was nowhere to be seen. Perhaps his father was making him kneel on the prayer mat for longer than usual to pray for safety from the plague.

So I ran to the gate and stuck my nose through the bars to watch the funeral processions. Half-naked men ran carrying litters and chanting: '*Ram! Ram! Sita! Ram!*' Bundles wrapped in white cloth bounced about on the litters as they ran. Ayah pulled me away. 'The dead will be burned by the Ganges, but there are too many to be burned properly, so the rats will get them. And you will have bad dreams.'

At bedtime, after Mummy had sung me my lullaby, kissed me goodnight, tucked in my mosquito net and gone to join Daddy on the verandah for their evening *chota-peg*, Ayah took over. She inspected under the bed to make sure no snake was curled up in the chamber pot. She assured me the howling jackals were too far away to harm us. Then she rolled herself into her quilted *resai*. 'And the tiger is in the jungle,' she said, 'waiting for the Sahib's bullet.'

She covered her head and lay down beside my bed. With Ayah I was safe.

Nora Naish

70 years ago my Gentile family lived in Upper Clapton, close to Stamford Hill, a predominantly Orthodox Jewish area. One day in 1939, I can remember my father, a City of London policeman, bringing an Orthodox Jewish husband and wife into our house and sitting them down.

He had been walking towards home after finishing his duties, still wearing his uniform, when he saw this elderly Jewish couple approaching him. Upon seeing him they stepped off the pavement into the gutter, the male removing his hat and both bowing their heads.

My father, being somewhat surprised, stopped and asked them why they did it. Although they were trembling with fear, they told him that where they came from if they didn't step into the gutter voluntarily, a uniformed policeman would have clubbed them into it. He took them gently by the hands, told them he meant them no harm and led them into our house. He told my mother what was happening and they sat down and had a cup of tea with them.

My father told them that in our free country it was a policeman's job to protect all citizens. The elderly couple broke down in tears and tried to kneel at his feet and bless him, but he stopped them. Can you imagine what effect all this had on me, a six-year-old? My father sent them on their way with good wishes and offering his assistance should they need his help. I can never remember him being so upset, not even later during the London Blitz when he saw terrible things.

John Miles

My father told them that in our free country it was a policeman's job to protect all citizens. The elderly Jewish couple broke down in tears

40 years ago I was waiting at a bus stop in Hemsworth, Yorkshire. It was raining heavily in the manner known locally as 'stair rods', and a number of us were waiting inside the shelter. Two older men were outside, seemingly oblivious to the rain running down their balding heads. They stood ramrod stiff, looking across the market-place deep in thought. One man broke the silence: 'It were a day like this when it were Passchendaele.' Those of us inside the shelter looked at each other with disbelief. After what seemed like an aeon, the other replied: 'Ay, tha's reet, Jack, it were a wet 'un.' The rain continued and silence returned.

Angus I MacIntosh

OLDIE MASTERS

A guide to neglected artists

Iain MacNab (1890–1967)

The Wine Cask

12x18 inches. Watercolour. Signed. Circa 1935.

MACNAB only began to train as an artist after being invalided out of the First World War.

He studied at the Glasgow School of Art, then Heatherleys, of which he became joint Principal, then spent time in Paris before returning to set up the Grosvenor School of Modern Art – birthplace of some of the best wood-engravers and, most famously, lino-cutters of the time.

While much of his workload was taken up with administration, he cut more than ninety very fine, formal wood engravings.

Many of his subjects are Mediterranean, and this watercolour, probably painted in Majorca in the 1930s, shows how well he could suggest mass and light.

PHILIP ATHILL

Above: Paul Hogarth's 'In Betjeman's Footsteps' *Oldie* cover, March 1996 (left) and his 'Majorca Revisited' *Oldie* cover from September 1995; facing page: illustration of Hidcote Manor, *The Oldie*, May 1995

Paul Hogarth

RICHARD INGRAMS pays tribute to the artist and illustrator whose work was celebrated in an exhibition in spring 2010

A retrospective exhibition featuring a variety of work by Paul Hogarth, who died in 2001 aged 84 after a long career as artist and illustrator, went on show at the Francis Kyle Gallery in London's Maddox Street on 10th March 2010. It included work that Paul did for *The Oldie* over a number of years.

After submitting an 'I Once Met' about Sir Paul Getty in 1992, Paul became a regular contributor to the magazine, both as artist and writer. Our main illustration shows Hidcote, famous for its garden, where Paul was a National Trust tenant and where he received an *Oldie* readers' outing led by our then gardening correspondent, Deborah Kellaway.

Highly professional, Paul was a model contributor who always met deadlines and never made a fuss. We were privileged to publish his outstanding illustrations, articles and covers.

Michael Heseltine

Sacked and snubbed, **EDWARD MIRZOEFF** *recalls his encounters with the Tory big beast*

Who was he – a Greek god? An officer of the Wehrmacht? Tarzan? Aged 17 and just arrived at Oxford from grammar school, I could not but be struck by that glamorous figure, tall and erect, with his swept-back golden hair and piercing pale-blue eyes, so imposing in the white tie and tails of the Treasurer of the Oxford Union. In 1954 Michael Heseltine was setting out to make an impression, and he succeeded.

The looks were not all. Heseltine's canny slogan: 'Four-course lunches, 2/6d, five-course dinners, 3/6d' brought impecunious undergraduates crowding into the Union. As President, he converted the old cellars into a nightclub, and a thousand new members joined. I never summoned up the courage to speak to the great man, but here, obviously, was an entrepreneur of the future.

Heseltine thought so too. After Oxford he teamed up with Clive Labovitch. Labovitch, a scion of the Leeds rag-trade, had bought the little Oxford magazine, *Cherwell*, and turned it into a weekly student newspaper. They seemed unlikely partners. 'With those two little pals of mine, Labovitch and Heseltine,' we sang, echoing a West Indian cricket calypso of the time.

But they were a success. What first brought in the money was their Cornmarket Press *Directory of Opportunities for Graduates*, a careers guide rich in potential for advertising revenue. Then came the magazines, particularly *Man About Town*, a title soon slimmed down to *About Town* and finally just *Town*. Smart, up-to-the-minute art direction, high-quality photo-journalism, and imaginative writing from Kingsley Amis, Ken Tynan and Tom Stoppard, among many other bright names, made for a heady mix of Sixties excitement and style.

My own career was less glittering. By 1962 I was in my third dead-end job as assistant editor of *Shoppers' Guide*, a small consumer magazine owned by the British Standards Institution. Staffed entirely by women, it was written in a chatty, homely and familiar style, like those in the many women's magazines of the period. Good homemaking was the key. The lead subject one month, I remember, was Ladies' Cardigans. Less fun than its publicity-conscious rival *Which?*, *Shoppers' Guide* did not give Best Buys, or even clear advice on particular goods, preferring to set out the facts and leave the decisions to its readers.

PHOTO COURTESY JOHN COLE/EVENING STANDARD/GETTY IMAGES

I could not but be struck by that glamorous figure, tall and erect, with his swept-back golden hair and piercing pale-blue eyes...

It was therefore with some surprise that I picked up the telephone one day to hear Michael Heseltine at the other end of the line, inviting me to lunch with him and Labovitch at a restaurant of a grandeur I had never previously encountered. Why did they want to spend money on me? It soon became clear. They had a mind to purchase *Shoppers' Guide*, smarten it up, and make it hugely profitable. I was to give them the

'Bursitis, Major. I'll give you a note excusing you from salutes'

inside information on which to base their bid. They hardly needed to offer a second glass of *premier cru*. It was an exciting prospect, and I was all for it. I gave what details I could.

Heseltine's bid succeeded. *Shoppers' Guide* was absorbed into the trendy Cornmarket Press, and soon emerged with a dramatic change of style. The cool young graphic designers went to town with new typefaces, startling layouts, different paper, even a strange new shape, turning the magazine on its side.

Our readers, the ladies in the shires, were not impressed. They began to cancel their subscriptions. I became worried about the way things were going, and made no effort to hide my dismay from my colleagues. Once again the phone rang with a summons to see Mr Heseltine – but this time in his office. He stared at me – those blue eyes! – then got straight to the point. Apparently the editor, a rather tiresome woman, had complained to him that I was spreading doom and disaffection in the ranks, even forecasting the closure of the magazine. He had no choice, he said, but to fire me. He added that I had misread the finances, and that the transformation was about to become a big success. Not so. Two months later *Shoppers' Guide* folded.

It was almost forty years before I saw Heseltine again, this time in Buckingham Palace. I was there to film a meeting of the Privy Council. Afterwards I told him that the last time we met he had sacked me. He replied, rather coldly, that he had no memory of me or of the occasion.

SHOPPING

ALICE PITMAN

PEARL'S HUTCH resembled something from an RSPCA poster. Costing £55 from a local pet shop five years ago, it was now a modern-day slum. The wire mesh had nearly caved in due to persistent ramming from foxes, the wooden shutters were half chewed by the dog, and the leaking roof had turned the interior mouldy and an area of fur on Pearl's back into dreadlocks. She never allowed this to get in the way of her appetite, however, growing so fat in the last year that once inside her hutch she had a job getting from her living room to her lavatory.

For months I had been staring out of the window at Pearl's ramshackle abode, and feeling guilty. What kind of an owner was I? The rabbit should have a new hutch. But new hutches are expensive. A cursory internet search revealed that for a rabbit of Pearl's dimensions they cost anything up to £175. And second-hand ones in the small ads always seem to get snapped up so quickly. Also, what if we forked out all that money only for her to die shortly afterwards? Rabbits aren't supposed to live very long and Pearl was getting on for six. Anyway, she spent all day roaming free in the garden and it was only the threat of predators that led her to being cooped up in an unsuitably-sized hutch at night. If wild rabbits could make do with cramped underground burrows, then Pearl was laughing.

But then visitors started commenting – 'She looks like that were-rabbit in *Wallace and Gromit*,' said the window cleaner. 'Can she actually fit in that? Aren't rabbits supposed to be able to stand up in their hutches?' – and shortly after Christmas, the dog leapt on top of the hutch and the roof caved in.

It was finally time to face up to my responsibility. Driving en-route to Purrfect for Pets in Leatherhead with son Fred and Mr Shopping, a marvellous thing happened: on the grass verge outside someone's house stood a very large rabbit hutch. A note attached read: 'Free, Please Take'. Unable to believe my luck, I executed a near-emergency stop, and leapt out of our old VW banger to inspect it. It was everything we could have hoped for: sturdy, spacious – ample for two rabbits really – good quality roofing and in very good nick: the perfect abode for Mama Cass, whom we had left on the patio munching her way through a large economy carrot from Tesco. Fred and I rather furtively secreted it in the boot of the car before any rival rabbit owners could stake their claim. I wondered what I should do with the 'Free, Please Take' sign. Mr Shopping, in the passenger seat listening to the cricket, suggested we attach it to their BMW and make off with that as well.

The new hutch is a real hit with Pearl, although public displays of appreciation are not really her style. She still thumps petulantly at every opportunity and hops off in the other direction if any of us make an overture of friendship. But I can tell she's secretly pleased with it. I have carpeted her ample living room with an old jumper (rabbit books say you should always line their hutches with plenty of hay, but this offends Pearl who pushes the lot out with her snout). Where the old hutch was open-plan, the new one has a stylish wooden partition between the living quarters and the toilet. It is a rabbit Graceland and, like Elvis, she likes nothing better than to sit in her jungle room stuffing her face with food all day. Pearl's weakness is popcorn (sugar-coated preferred), toast, and her favourite herb, flat-leaf parsley. When she's not eating, she stares at nothing for ages.

Even though she doesn't really like us, and is in turn quite boring, we've grown strangely fond of her. In fact, the patio wouldn't be the same without the fat cow. The morning when I find her conked out on her toilet with a mouthful of popcorn in her gob will be a sad one.

FREEDOM Pass-times

ROBERT LOW *becomes a Tai Chi Master*

Illustrated by **ROGER FEREDAY**

My joints are getting pretty creaky, the legacy of a lifetime playing sport of all types. I've had five knee operations, suffer from constant lower-back pain and now have an arthritic hip. Short of a body transplant, how can I retain a reasonable amount of mobility?

A friend said Tai Chi, the ancient Chinese martial art, had done wonders for his arthritis. Indeed, an article he wrote about it for the magazine where I used to work prompted the biggest postbag for years from older readers, so there was clearly a lot of interest out there.

Like most people, I suspect, the only thing I had seen of Tai Chi were television clips of elderly Chinese making slow, graceful gestures and movements, a bit like ballet in slow motion, in the open air. When a flyer advertising classes dropped through our door, I acted. At 6.30 pm the following Tuesday I turned up at a church hall in West Hampstead to be greeted by Karim, the instructor, a tall, powerful-looking young man with a commanding presence. It cost a £50 annual fee and £9 per lesson.

There were about ten of us, including three women. Most seemed quite experienced, wearing black T-shirts emblazoned with Chinese lettering and the outline of a bird, symbol of Fujian White Crane Tai Chi, the particular speciality to which the group belongs, and baggy black trousers. Some had yellow or red sashes, which denoted higher grades. I was the oldest by about thirty years but was immediately made to feel welcome. Although a complete beginner, I was filtered straight into the group – but Karim, having heard a brief rundown of my medical history, kept a close eye on me, made sure I didn't overdo things and occasionally asked a more experienced pupil to show me the ropes. After each such interlude, my helper would bow courteously before rejoining the group.

Somewhat to my surprise, a lot of the hour-long class was spent doing stretching exercises, the idea being, I presume, that you need to be fit and flexible before you can embark on Tai Chi proper. To my great relief there was a total absence of spiritual mumbo-jumbo: the whole thing was very pragmatic and quite hard work. After half an hour, we came to the first and most basic Tai Chi

Halfway through my first exercise I felt my wretched trousers unravel and start to descend towards my knees

routine, the nine steps. 'Horse stance!' bellowed Karim (I thought at first he said 'horse dance' and wondered what on earth was coming), which means

standing in a semi-crouch with the legs apart, as if riding a horse, and then doing nine moves around a notional nine-square grid.

I enjoyed the class enough to go back for more. Karim suggested I buy the White Crane black T-shirt and trousers, which were extraordinary. They have an enormous waist, like a clown's trousers, which, Karim explained, you gather in, folding to right and left before rolling over several times to tighten. This I did, or so I thought, but halfway through my first exercise I felt the wretched things unravel and start to descend towards my knees. Blushing furiously, I pulled them up but the same thing happened again. Karim kindly interrupted his instructing to show me where I was going wrong: I was rolling the waist in, not out. My trousers have stayed up since, thank goodness.

I'm now a regular, and my nine steps are going well enough for me to try out a Sunday morning class over in Islington taught by Dennis Ngo, White Crane's chief instructor and a Master of the art. This class was to teach the basics of *suang yang*, the next stage after the nine steps. We spent the best part of 45 minutes learning one 21-movement sequence involving a few simple bends and twists, and a faux martial arts crouch. The Master, who grew up in Singapore, made it look incredibly graceful. He was rather terrifying at first, barking out orders and exhibiting some impatience with our slowness, but softened up as the class wore on.

It's early days, but I'm now doing stretching exercises and my nine steps every morning, and my aches and pains do seem to have eased already. Dennis and Karim are taking a group of about sixty students to China to learn at the feet of Fujian masters in the homeland. 'You should come next year,' said Karim encouragingly. I just might.

Canary Wharf

Smelly, soul destroying and divisive – but at least it's got a Waitrose

NIGEL REYNOLDS *reports*

The visitor arriving at Canary Wharf by car is not likely to be prepared for the olfactory shock. The subterranean roundabout that is the motorist's main gateway to London's multi-billion pound 'model working environment for the 21st century' quite literally stinks. It is the cloying, gagging, clothes-permeating stink of gallons of hot cooking oil. Should you be stuck in traffic on this Guernica of a roundabout, two or three minutes are enough to induce a state of serious panic.

It is one misfortune that the vents from the kitchens of a five-star hotel were designed to extract their pong directly onto the public below. It is a second, more serious one, and emblematic of the con trick that is Canary Wharf, that the first impression and last memory each day for thousands of workers and visitors is of this oxygen-lite hell hole.

One small lie is that this great new finance district is only fifteen minutes from London. It might just be when the hopelessly unreliable Jubilee Line and toytown light railway are working, but, in truth, most trips to London take the best part of 45 minutes.

Canary Wharf is a cut-off place of 22-carat artifice – an eleven-million-square-foot marble and glass banking and shopping park occupied round-the-clock by 90,000-plus banker worker ants protected by gates from the real world. Physically detached from reality in a sterile dream-world of computer screens, expensive shops, restaurants and gyms, perhaps it is not surprising that the bankers, fund-managers and analysts of Canary Wharf all gradually went mad and stretched the world's debt this way and that until it went into meltdown.

No public road runs through Canary Wharf (the same mistake was made with 1960s council estates) and private security men police the 97-acre 'estate', regulating behaviour – smoking, for example, is not allowed in the streets.

Much worse, however, is that Canary Wharf's 800-foot towers stand like twinkling candelabra over some of the worst pockets of deprivation in the country. Although the Wharf was intended to regenerate the wastelands of E14, the bankers went out of their way to lock out the unwashed. For many years – the management has now, I think, been shamed into dropping the practice – entrances to the shopping malls carried euphemistic notices advising: 'No working clothes or boots allowed inside.'

This apartheid was encapsulated in an incident six years ago when the Wharf, anxious to protect the sushi restaurants and expensive emporia selling brie and grape sandwiches, attempted to evict Bene Bene, the only down-to-earth snack shop in the place. Its crime was to sell baked beans, bacon sandwiches and Mars bars at honest prices. With 4,000 customers a day it was hugely popular, but the Canary Wharf Group maintained that it had broken its contract requiring it to be a healthfood restaurant. There was an outcry and Bene Bene fortunately won the day.

Odd things happen when normal values are distorted. During one of the many security scares at Canary Wharf, cars entering the car parks were held in long queues while each one was searched for bombs. One frustrated colleague, on reaching the checkpoint, was asked what his business was. He said that he was going to Waitrose. He was waived through with a smile: 'Waitrose! Oh, that's fine. No need to check you.'

But the strangest thing about this dump is that it is not really a monument to the glories of free enterprise at all. In 2000 the Department for the Environment computed the cost to the public of constructing Canary Wharf. With the clean-up costs of the land, transport improvements and 'enterprise zone' tax breaks and grants, it transpired that the taxpayer had handed over £4 billion: £4 for every £1 put in by the developers.

PHOTOGRAPH COURTESY © KAYE KERR/ISTOCKPHOTO.COM

Akenfield at forty

2009 marked the fortieth anniversary of the publication of Ronald Blythe's *Akenfield: Portrait of an English Village.* **PAUL BARNES** talked to the author about the book and the cult film that it inspired

Nobody had heard of Akenfield until Ronald Blythe coined the name to mask two real Suffolk villages that he was writing about.

In the mid-Sixties, Penguin Books and their American opposite number, Pantheon, suddenly saw virtue in recording the changing patterns of rural life. Their editors' remit was worldwide, and writers were commissioned to chronicle these changes in countries other than their own. 'They used to send a Pole to Russia or a Frenchmen to Tripoli to write something interesting and original,' says Blythe. 'But when it came to me they said "Oh, you do something in Britain."'

He saw no need to stray far from home. Suffolk born and bred, he was living in an old farmhouse at Debach, a tiny village of about eighty people near Woodbridge. A little farther along the old Roman road is the slightly larger village of Charsfield, with St Peter's Church in the middle. Blythe served there as churchwarden and knew nearly everybody around – farm workers, schoolteachers, the vet and the blacksmith, the rural dean and the gravedigger. He set about interviewing them with their accounts of village life, past and present.

'I seemed to have some effect, when I talked to them about life and farming, which made them at ease with me,' he says. 'I did know about bell-ringing and ploughing, and hundreds of country things about flowers, so I wasn't asking questions as much as just listening to fragments about their lives.'

He began with the district nurse, Marjorie Jope, 'a rather tough woman, imposing and difficult'. She was real enough but, like every other person in Blythe's book,

Scenes from Peter Hall's film *Akenfield*: haymaking (left) and ploughing (below). Right: Ronald Blythe (left) and Peter Hall during the filming

her name is his invention. She came to the village in 1925 with aspirins, torn sheets for bandages and a salary of £2 per week. Before her arrival in Akenfield, births and deaths were the province of 'secretive old women'. At first the village kept its secrets from her, but gradually people grew to trust her. 'She became a person of great power, really,' says Blythe. 'People respected her so much.'

Long after the book was published he got to know her very well, but all those years earlier, she never made it easy for him. 'She didn't give me confidence at all,' he says, 'but she made the book serious, I think. I knew what I'd got to do in this book.'

He decided to divide it between three generations, separated by the two world wars, beginning with what the oldest men could recall of their childhood at the end of the nineteenth century – a time when the land all about them was changing hands; wheat, barley and beet were giving ground to orchards of plums and pears, or grass; ingenious farm machinery was emerging from factories in Ipswich and Leiston; and tractors were taking over from horses.

When the Great War ended, Horry, the saddler, was still a boy. He started as an apprentice for sixpence a week, rising to a shilling when he was fourteen, eventually buying the business. 'Our harness lasted forever,' he told Blythe. 'It was our downfall! We made these things so well that they did us out of a living.' Horry remembered the first combine harvester arriving in Akenfield, just after World War Two. 'It was one of those things you could only use on nice, fine days,' he said, 'and you couldn't cut barley with it, only wheat. Now they are everywhere and the horses are quite gone.'

Derek the ploughman was born as the Thirties ended. When Blythe wrote his book Derek was the Akenfield ploughman: 'Fields which once engaged dozens of horse teams and even quite a number of tractor-drivers nowadays see nobody but him.' He was alone most of his working time, but never felt lonely.

Akenfield reads like a series of monologues, as though its subjects spoke verbatim, without prompting. 'Oh, a lot of it is verbatim,' Blythe says, 'but the book isn't a lot of tape recordings. *I wrote the book.* I made something of their lives from what I knew as a Suffolk person, and what I knew of their position, socially and in history.'

'I made something of their lives from what I knew as a Suffolk person, and what I knew of their position, socially and in history'

He delivered the finished manuscript, went home and waited. It took nearly two years before he was back in the West End for Penguin's launch. 'I was amazed,' he says. 'They'd got nets hanging up on the wall and ceiling, threaded with flowers and corn and things, very rustic. It was astonishing.'

So were the reviews. Angus Wilson called it 'a penetrating, extraordinarily unprejudiced, yet deeply caring account of modern rural life in England.' John Updike declared it 'exquisite'. Sales were astonishing too, though many must have bought the book in the mistaken belief that it would satisfy some nostalgic longing. 'Like an idyll,' says Blythe, 'rather like Flora Thompson. But she's not nostalgic. She's very truthful.'

One reader struck by the truth of *Akenfield* was the director Peter Hall, another Suffolk boy, born in Bury St Edmund's. He bought the rights to film it, using only local amateur actors, with a screenplay written by Blythe.

It had its premiere on 26 January 1975, showing simultaneously at the Paris Pullman cinema in London and on ITV. The reviews were spattered with words like 'exceptional', 'beautiful', 'lyrical' and 'magical'. Kenneth Tynan noted in his diary that 'P Hall's mastery of public relations surges relentlessly on: for weeks now it's been impossible to turn on the radio or TV or pick up a paper without reading something radiant about his film of *Akenfield*.'

Both the book and the film generated their small share of pilgrims who beat a path to the 'real' Akenfield. They still turn up, but not often, according to Martin Tilbury at The Three Horseshoes. Apart from a handful of old photographs in his bar, and St Peter's Church round the corner, there is little to see. Charsfield and Debach are not exactly picturesque, though the countryside is pleasing enough. It's hard to imagine an 'Akenfield trail' as a marketing concept.

'You're not likely, after all this time, to bump into any of the people that were in the book,' says Maggie Jennings. 'And anyway you wouldn't recognise them.' She once ran a B&B in the farmhouse where the book was written, placing a copy, Gideon-like, in every room. Blythe's study became the 'Akenfield Suite', and a farm nearby supplied 'Akenfield Eggs', free-range of course. It didn't last. The house became a private family home, and you won't find Akenfield Eggs in any directory.

Blythe lives in another old farmhouse now, well away from the nearest road. He says that when the book came out he did worry a little about what some of the people in it might think. 'I went in to the village shop after the hullabaloo,' he says. 'An old lady, the widow of a farmer, came to her gate and beckoned, and I thought "I'm for it". I walked across and she said, "Oh, my dear, you should have come to me. I could have told you much worse than that." And then I felt safe in a way.'

Readers write

Oldie readers are an articulate bunch. Here's a selection of letters from the Oldie Towers postbag

Declaring our genius

SIR: Your correspondents express various views about the content of your magazine, but I have yet to see mention of the one feature for which, on its own, I would cheerfully pay my £2.95 – Antico's Genius Crossword.

Crosswords have been around for donkey's years, but once one has mastered the basic approach, even the best become fairly routine. Antico, however, with his 'unclued entries', 'missing letters', and the requirement for some knowledge of poetry, literature or whatever, has moved into a new generation of puzzle. He has single-handedly developed 'son of crossword'. It is the high spot of my month.
John Brisbourne, Dorking, Surrey

Death by a thousand cuts

SIR: I have today cancelled my direct debit to your magazine. I said the next time there were numerous pages dedicated to book reviews I would cancel, and so I have.
D D Howard, by email

Nothing better to do

SIR: Dogs Trust is a registered charity concerned with the care and welfare of dogs. The slogan 'A Dog is for Life not just for Christmas ®' was devised by Dogs Trust over twenty years ago and has since been a major part of our seasonal promotional campaigns to raise awareness of the serious issue of the abandonment and mistreatment of dogs, and in our fundraising and educational activities generally. Dogs Trust has built up and now owns a valuable goodwill and reputation in the well-known slogan which has become a registered trademark belonging to Dogs Trust.

It has come to our attention that in your latest edition you have used the slogan 'A BOOK IS FOR LIFE NOT JUST FOR CHRISTMAS'. Please note that any use or adaptation of our registered trademark requires prior express permission from Dogs Trust. This charity aims to stop all unauthorised use of any of its registered trademarks and copyright and you are kindly requested to cease using the slogan 'A BOOK IS FOR LIFE NOT JUST FOR CHRISTMAS'.
Chrissie Paphiti, solicitor on behalf of Dogs Trust

Red mist

SIR: I am so glad I decided not to renew my subscription to *The Oldie*. Your ignorant and irresponsible rant regarding red kites entirely justifies my decision.
Jackie Coulson, Wakefield

Forced labour of love

SIR: Thank you for *The Oldie*. Before retirement the only magazines I ever read were the Sunday supplements or lurid glossies in the hairdressers. Then I enrolled on a writing course and was forced to study magazines in depth. I found *The Oldie* and regret all the previous issues I have missed.

It is probably naïve to admit I enjoy reading it. Most of your correspondents seem very scathing. Perhaps continued study will teach me to be more critical.
Linda Jones, Gloucester

Better prospects elsewhere

SIR: Thank you for your two letters, 1st and 29th November respectively, telling me that my annual subscription runs out very soon. In reply I have to tell you that I shall not renew it.

I very much like a lot of your contributors' articles but, having been with your magazine almost from the start, I still cannot stand 'East of Islington', your own television review or Mavis Nicholson. I also find the cartoons are usually badly drawn, pointless or downright vulgar.

Another perhaps minor point concerns grammatical errors. For example, in your reminder letter, first paragraph, you say '....cartoon book *for free*' (my italics). Something may be 'free' or 'for nothing' – never 'for free'. It grates most harshly.

So, for the above reasons, I have had enough and hereby cancel my membership from the end of this year's subscription, preferring to transfer my affection to *Prospect*, an excellent monthly magazine that I would fully recommend. The cartoons are good, too.
H C T Routley, Bournemouth

Floored

SIR: I live on the top floor of a block of flats with locks on the main entrance remotely operated from individual flats. My flat has a lobby outside of my front door in which I laid an expensive oriental rug in 2007.

Some months later the rug was stolen, but fourteen months afterwards it reappeared. After a few months it was again stolen – but even more amazingly was once more returned about four months later. This sequence of events has left me quite baffled. Should any of your readers have a theory explaining these strange events I would be delighted to hear from them.
David Radford, Hove

Top toons

SIR: In each new *Oldie* my wife and I go straight to the cartoons and share a happy half-hour chuckling at the recession-breaking humour. We've gone a step further and mounted photocopies on a large pin-board so we can have a good laugh every day to keep the blues at bay.
Gilberte and Stanley Lover, via email

'I note with great sorrow that you have sent me a large brown envelope containing a horrid little magazine'

Top chump

SIR: Like many others, I don't see the point of the 'Top Chumps'. It seems to be in the current negative vein of 'knock the successful in others' (by some anonymous, probably jealous, back-room nobody) when you run out of positive ideas yourself. I have to agree that I am not particularly impressed with some of the people that you try to ridicule but at least they have succeeded in doing something positive for themselves. I have great respect for Mr Ingrams but I am sure there would be many who would happily contribute to a Top Chumps on him, given the (very unlikely) chance. Please, let us get back to features which are interesting, informative and show positive fair play.
Ian Frame, via email

Bag of crap

SIR: I note with great sorrow that you have once again sent me a large brown envelope containing a horrid little magazine. You seem to do this every month. I cannot begin to imagine why. I have never asked you to, nor ever paid you anything for it.

I am constantly bombarded with free shit for no reason I can properly understand, and I have decided to clamp down on it. Send me your vile, bigoted, humourless, bag-of-crap publication again, and I shall be forced to call the police.
Giles Coren, London

EXPAT

JOHN MOORE

Chiang Mai, Thailand

THE OTHER DAY I was rushed to the local hospital, an experience from which, happily, both I and the Thai emergency medical services emerged relatively unscathed. Things started recently when I was catching moths in the hills and suddenly felt a furious beating of wings inside my right ear. I attempted to extract the intruder with a selection of toothpicks, chopsticks, barbecue skewers and, in desperation, a screwdriver, without success. Abandoning the nearest health centre, where an unsympathetic nurse ordered me to wait behind two thousand colourfully-costumed tribespeople clutching babies for vaccination, I proceeded to the next town and found a smart new hospital with a group of immaculately-attired nurses enjoying spicy papaya salad outside. The A & E was deserted apart from an elderly lady wielding a mop. The staff would return from lunch in around an hour. Probably. I could have been hacked to within millimetres of my life by an axe-wielding maniac, but I would still have to wait while the nurses finished their *somtam*.

Eventually, a doctor who had finished his lunch obligingly shone a small torch into my ear. Then a high-powered flashlight. Finally he tried a different pair of glasses. 'No insect in ear. Jus crotty brud.' Not convinced, I found a supply of cotton buds and undertook daily excavations for any arthropodal remains, which is how a cotton tip parted company with its stick and became dislodged somewhere inside my *meatus acusticus*.

I was whisked to our nearest hospital, and explained my predicament to a receptionist cleverly concealed in a dark corridor under a sign saying 'BEWARE YOUR HEAD'. Recognising the urgency of the situation, she handed me a 24-page form printed in arcane Thai script on brown blotting-paper with questions on the Thai Constitution, what my grandparents had for breakfast and whom to contact in the event of my demise. Blood pressure, temperature and weight laboriously measured, there ensued an earnest discussion on the correct Thai spelling of 'cotton bud'.

Waiting outside the examination room, I noticed that the doctor was sitting completely still, apparently lifeless. Dead doctors? Not a good sign. Meanwhile a fellow patient quizzed me with typical female Thai delicacy on my age, salary, marital situation, disinclination to have more children, had I been sterilised and did I need a housekeeper. Then somehow the doctor revived and with the aid of a candle and an oxyacetylene torch (I made that bit up) located the offending piece of cotton. After a fascinating lecture on the human auditory system, he sent me to A & E where it would be removed. They had, he ominously informed me, better equipment there.

Surrounded by recumbent bodies bristling with tubes as in some nightmarish experiment, a comely nurse fetched a toolkit of variously sized toasting forks and began prodding. Suddenly a thunderbolt of pain shot through me. Instinctively, I grabbed the nearest thing that came to hand, which happened to be the nurse's left breast. With a shrill squeal (which I assumed at the time to be one of delight though, on reflection, could have been surprise) she shot about six feet in the air, to the astonishment of the supine patients and their anxious relatives. Removing the tip proved straightforward – one nurse held the torch, one wielded the tongs while the third held me down and the fourth shouted encouragement. My ear finally clear of the obstruction, I was able to return to my moths and the nurses to correcting each others' spelling unmolested.

Doing nothing puts you under a lot of pressure

Meeting the Mahatma

In 1944 **ANNE PIPER** *made the arduous pilgrimage to the centre of India to interview Gandhi in his ashram. But when her moment came, she became rather tongue-tied...*

In October 1944 I was working for All India Radio in Delhi. I had read Gandhi's autobiography and very much admired his philosophy of *ahimsa*, or non-violence. I wrote asking for a meeting.

Gandhi had chosen the location of the ashram at Sevagram by putting a pin in the centre of a map of India. Wardha, the nearest town, was about five miles away. The train from Delhi ran only once a day and it took 26 hours to make the journey. I arrived at the ashram in the dark after a very long tonga ride beside flooded fields. It was damp and chilly.

I was met at the gate by an old man with a lantern who took me to join the communal prayers, which were being held that night on a verandah because of the rains. The service was ecumenical, with readings from many religions. Gandhi liked Christian hymns, particularly 'When I Survey the Wondrous Cross', which he liked to sing when he was in jail.

At the end of the prayers I was led up to Gandhi, who said: 'At last you have come, you have found your way to this Godforsaken place.' We started to walk towards his house and he remarked, 'Oh dear, there are a terrible lot of snakes and scorpions here, but you must not be afraid of them.' I reminded him that he admitted in his autobiography to being frightened of them too. Yes, it was quite true, he said, but he was a terrible coward. He told me: 'Tonight I want you to rest; tomorrow is my day of silence, but you will be able to go around and see everything. On the next day we can talk.'

IMAGE COURTESY POPPERFOTO/GETTY IMAGES

"Every evening Gandhi sat on the floor with a small Indian spinning-wheel and spun for half an hour"

The next day I got up at six o'clock in order to follow Gandhi on his morning walk, which started at seven. He leant on two small boys and about twenty people straggled after him. A deputation had come from the north to consult him, and they talked and talked, but as it was his day of silence he only smiled and nodded.

Afterwards I was taken on a tour of the ashram. We went first to the dispensary. Gandhi's secretary and nephew, Pyarelal, was using the verandah as an office and dictating to a typist. Inside, his sister, Dr Sushila Nayar, was attending to the patients who came daily for help and medicine from the surrounding villages. Sevagram is in a low-lying, malarial area and there was much work for her there.

Next we visited Gandhi's own house. He was out, taking a bath, so we looked at everything. There was nothing in the main room, where he ate and received everyone, except a mattress on the floor and a bookcase with about fifty books in it, including the *Concise Oxford Dictionary*. Among his few ornaments were the three 'See No Evil...' monkeys. In an alcove above his head was an Indian illuminated text which translated meant 'O God'. On another wall was a picture of Christ.

Then we visited the ashram kitchens. All the cooking was on wood fires, using wood collected from the nearby jungle. The place was self-supporting, and their cows gave better milk than I had tasted in Delhi.

The general ashram lunch was at twelve noon. About 25 people sat cross-legged on the verandah in two lines facing each other. The food was boiled mixed vegetables, mainly pumpkin, beans, a pinch of salt (none in the cooking), some raw onion, salad leaves, two sorts of wheat bread, and butter. The evening meal at six o'clock was much the same.

Later that afternoon I was taken to see the sacrificial spinning. Every evening Gandhi sat on the floor with a small Indian spinning-wheel and spun for half an hour. He liked to point out that India could be self-sufficient if Indians spun their own cotton and wool. Then he set out on his evening walk with fifty followers.

'Our newest model comes with a built-in hidden compartment for your life savings'

On his morning walk the next day Gandhi was far from silent. He transacted business, discussed important matters with men from Delhi, and received a Sikh deputation from the Punjab. On the way home he talked to me. He was afraid I must find it uncomfortable in the guest-house as he refused to provide mirrors for his guests. So I told him it was much more comfortable than I had expected it to be after reading the journalist Louis Fischer's account of eating boiled spinach on a visit. He started to give me a lesson in Hindi, making me repeat phrases after him. We went to visit a little girl who was ill in bed. Gandhi visited invalids in the ashram daily. I asked him, in my limited Hindi, if the child was very ill, but didn't understand a word of his long reply.

In the afternoon I was due to interview him. I sat down beside him on the mattress in his hut, and he turned round and looked at me. We both laughed and he said, 'You know you are supposed to ask me questions.' I said, 'I know, but I can't think of any.' He said, 'That is splendid,' and went on in Hindi: 'Shall I give you a Hindustani lesson?' I said yes, but then I thought I'd better say something sensible, so I said my visit was more like a visit he and a friend had once paid to Cardinal Manning. That pleased him and he said, 'You remember that?' We talked about Cardinal Manning and about London. In 1896, when he was a law student, Gandhi used to live in Store Street, just across the road from Percy Street, where I lived. He remembered Percy Street very well. As far as I remember, nothing else happened. Gandhi said later he had been quite willing to prolong our official interview, only I'd said I didn't want to. He described me as a 'good girl', which pleased me.

"I sat down beside Gandhi on the mattress in his hut, and he turned round and looked at me: 'You know you are supposed to ask me questions'"

Just before supper a baby was given a first birthday party outside Gandhi's hut. The main feature was a distribution of bananas to all the children. The baby disliked being garlanded, so the flowers were hung round the schoolmaster's daughter instead. It was a happy scene: Gandhi on his doorstep in the sun, the baby in its mother's arms beside him, an enormous basket of bananas at his feet, the children coming up in turn to get their share, everyone laughing.

After supper I sat on the step of the verandah watching a young Indian Communist trying to convert Gandhi. At the time the Indian Communists were in favour of fighting alongside Russia to show they were really on the side of the anti-fascist forces. Gandhi, however, said, 'Let him come by all means, stay as long as he likes, and try to convert me if he likes. If, however, by any chance I should happen to convert him, I am not responsible.'

Later that evening I went to say goodbye to Gandhi. He was talking to one man while another pulled the cord for his fan. A hurricane lamp on a stool beside him made his big steel spectacles glitter. There were four or five other people in the room sitting against the wall in the shadows. I sat on the doorstep at the end of Gandhi's mattress watching him for about ten minutes, as usual having no idea what was being said. He was an active speaker, gesticulating and laughing a lot. He had trouble with his shoulder cloth which kept slipping down and getting in his way.

He was glad I was leaving in a tonga rather than a bullock cart, saying, 'There is no brutality to animals here, you know.' I asked if he thought I was too heavy for two bullocks and he said, 'No, but they get so tired, our poor bullocks.' The tonga arrived and I left in good time to catch the only train to Delhi.

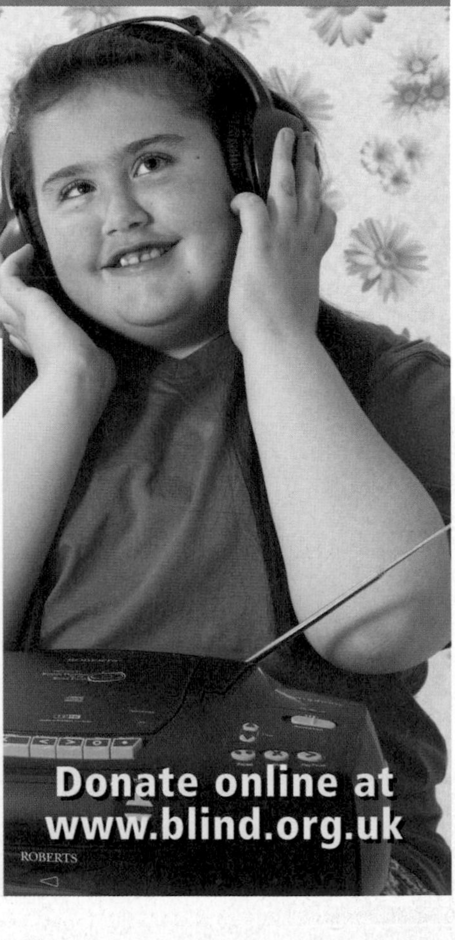

Genius crossword 255 *by Antico*

Each of fourteen clues comprises a definition part and a hidden consecutive jumble of the answer's letters including one extra letter; the extras spell out the three-word title of a work by a person whose surname is the answer to a clue without a definition part. The work's title also describes an occasion, the name of which occupies one row in the grid. In eight clues, cryptic indications are incomplete; in each case, the part of the answer not cryptically indicated is supplied by the occasion's name, treated as suggested by the second word of the work's title.

Across

1 Sympathise about love with operatic heroine missing one (11)
7 Fix home after pressure (3)
9 Obvious occasion consuming one day (7)
10 Coterie acclaiming patron saint of music (7)
11 High tension around scenes of operations (8)
12 Worker perhaps in wood reversing role (6)
13 Transformed ship steered round objects (9)
17 Drawn into a guess (5)
18 Misanthrope can set about doctor (5)
19 Campers told to avoid fungus (9)
21 Elder trees in outskirts (6)
22 Cheap area for passengers for example rejected (8)
26 Artist, hot in extra leather (7)
27 Meditation regarding psalm (7)
28 Unemotional demand by receiver (3)
29 Magnifies unknown article inside oval object (11)

Down

1 Hundred forms (7)
2 Kibbutz meal including cereal (5)
3 Forgotten episode lacking skill (5)
4 Be occupied by amendment of term for fanatic (9)
5 Curved structure with fracture (4)
6 Trades are suspended with endless surfeit around (9)
7 Stop trouble in committee (9)
8 Closest competition's ending (7)
14 Dynasty covered by hack over a year (9)
15 Make haphazard gestures in drama, overacting (9)
16 Unexpected acid in pitch (9)
18 Leader of demo immobilised with stun gun (7)
20 Character in *Hamlet* left (7)
23 Go into main street (5)
24 Take part after fuss (5)
25 Cheese diet at first (4)

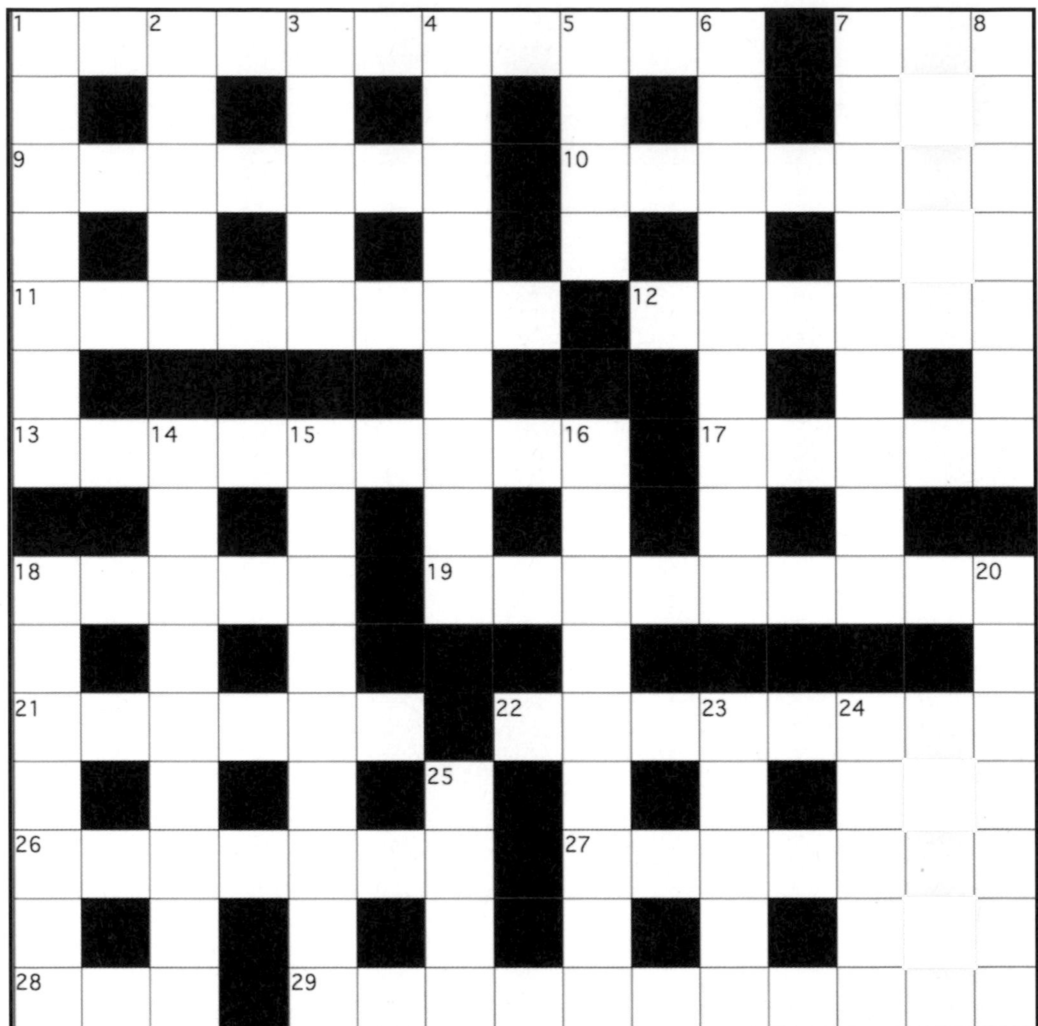